ICAS 2018

The Fourteenth International Conference on Autonomic and Autonomous Systems

May 20 - 24, 2018

Nice, France

ICAS 2018 Editors

Irina Topalova, FaGEEIM, Technical University Sofia, Bulgaria
Alina Trifan, University of Aveiro, Portugal
Antonio José Ribeiro Neves, University of Aveiro, Portugal

Printed from e-media with permission by:

Curran Associates, Inc.
57 Morehouse Lane
Red Hook, NY 12571

proceedings.com

Some format issues inherent in the e-media version may also appear in this print version.

Printed by Curran Associates, Inc. (2018)

International Academy, Research, and Industry Association (IARIA)
412 Derby Way
Wilmington, DE 19810

Phone: (408) 893-6407
Fax: (408) 527-6351

petre@iaria.org

Additional copies of this publication are available from:

Curran Associates, Inc.
57 Morehouse Lane
Red Hook, NY 12571 USA
Phone: 845-758-0400
Fax: 845-758-2633
Email: curran@proceedings.com
Web: www.proceedings.com

Table of Contents

ICAS 2018

Foreword

The Fourteenth International Conference on Autonomic and Autonomous Systems (ICAS 2018), held between May 20 - 24, 2018 - Nice, France, was a multi-track event covering related topics on theory and practice on systems automation, autonomous systems and autonomic computing.

The main tracks referred to the general concepts of systems automation, and methodologies and techniques for designing, implementing and deploying autonomous systems. The next tracks developed around design and deployment of context-aware networks, services and applications, and the design and management of self-behavioral networks and services. We also considered monitoring, control, and management of autonomous self-aware and context-aware systems and topics dedicated to specific autonomous entities, namely, satellite systems, nomadic code systems, mobile networks, and robots. It has been recognized that modeling (in all forms this activity is known) is the fundamental for autonomous subsystems, as both managed and management entities must communicate and understand each other. Small-scale and large-scale virtualization and model-driven architecture, as well as management challenges in such architectures are considered. Autonomic features and autonomy requires a fundamental theory behind and solid control mechanisms. These topics gave credit to specific advanced practical and theoretical aspects that allow subsystem to expose complex behavior. We aimed to expose specific advancements on theory and tool in supporting advanced autonomous systems. Domain case studies (policy, mobility, survivability, privacy, etc.) and specific technology (wireless, wireline, optical, e-commerce, banking, etc.) case studies were targeted. A special track on mobile environments was indented to cover examples and aspects from mobile systems, networks, codes, and robotics.

Pervasive services and mobile computing are emerging as the next computing paradigm in which infrastructure and services are seamlessly available anywhere, anytime, and in any format. This move to a mobile and pervasive environment raises new opportunities and demands on the underlying systems. In particular, they need to be adaptive, self-adaptive, and context-aware.

Adaptive and self-management context-aware systems are difficult to create, they must be able to understand context information and dynamically change their behavior at runtime according to the context. Context information can include the user location, his preferences, his activities, the environmental conditions and the availability of computing and communication resources. Dynamic reconfiguration of the context-aware systems can generate inconsistencies as well as integrity problems, and combinatorial explosion of possible variants of these systems with a high degree of variability can introduce great complexity.

Traditionally, user interface design is a knowledge-intensive task complying with specific domains, yet being user friendly. Besides operational requirements, design recommendations refer to standards of the application domain or corporate guidelines.

Commonly, there is a set of general user interface guidelines; the challenge is due to a need for cross-team expertise. Required knowledge differs from one application domain to another, and the core knowledge is subject to constant changes and to individual perception and skills.

Passive approaches allow designers to initiate the search for information in a knowledge-database to make accessible the design information for designers during the design process. Active approaches, e.g., constraints and critics, have been also developed and tested. These mechanisms deliver information (critics) or restrict the design space (constraints) actively, according to the rules and guidelines. Active and passive approaches are usually combined to capture a useful user interface design.

We take here the opportunity to warmly thank all the members of the ICAS 2018 Technical Program Committee, as well as the numerous reviewers. The creation of such a high quality conference program would not have been possible without their involvement. We also kindly thank all the authors who dedicated much of their time and efforts to contribute to ICAS 2018. We truly believe that, thanks to all these efforts, the final conference program consisted of top quality contributions.

Also, this event could not have been a reality without the support of many individuals, organizations, and sponsors. We are grateful to the members of the ICAS 2018 organizing committee for their help in handling the logistics and for their work to make this professional meeting a success.

We hope that ICAS 2018 was a successful international forum for the exchange of ideas and results between academia and industry and for the promotion of progress in the fields of autonomic and autonomous systems.

We are convinced that the participants found the event useful and communications very open. We also hope that Nice provided a pleasant environment during the conference and everyone saved some time for exploring this beautiful city.

ICAS 2018 Chairs:

ICAS Steering Committee

Satoshi Kurihara, University of Electro-Communications, Japan
Ljubo Vlacic, Griffith University, Australia
Roy Sterritt, Ulster University, UK
Mark J. Balas, Embry-Riddle Aeronautical University, USA
Elisabetta Di Nitto, Politecnico di Milano, Italy
Radu Calinescu, University of York, UK
Karsten Böhm, Fachhochschule Kufstein, Austria
S.G. Ponnambalam, Monash University Malaysia, Malaysia
Richard Anthony, University of Greenwich, UK
Jacques Malenfant, UPMC, France
Wladyslaw Homenda, Warsaw University of Technology, Poland
Albert M. K. Cheng, University of Houston, USA

ICAS Industry/Research Advisory Committee

Loris Penserini, Informatica e Società Digitale - IES, Italy
Stefanos Vrochidis, Centre for Research and Technology Hellas - Thermi-Thessaloniki, Greece
Tsuyoshi Ide, IBM T. J. Watson Research Center, USA
Petr Skobelev, Knowledge Genesis Group / Samara Technical University, Russia
Rajat Mehrotra, Intelligent Automation Inc., USA
Andreas Kercek, Lakeside Labs GmbH, Austria
Claudius Stern, biozoom services GmbH - Kassel | FOM University of Applied Sciences - Essen, Germany

ICAS 2018

Committee

ICAS Steering Committee

Satoshi Kurihara, University of Electro-Communications, Japan
Ljubo Vlacic, Griffith University, Australia
Roy Sterritt, Ulster University, UK
Mark J. Balas, Embry-Riddle Aeronautical University, USA
Elisabetta Di Nitto, Politecnico di Milano, Italy
Radu Calinescu, University of York, UK
Karsten Böhm, Fachhochschule Kufstein, Austria
S.G. Ponnambalam, Monash University Malaysia, Malaysia
Richard Anthony, University of Greenwich, UK
Jacques Malenfant, UPMC, France
Wladyslaw Homenda, Warsaw University of Technology, Poland
Albert M. K. Cheng, University of Houston, USA

ICAS Industry/Research Advisory Committee

Loris Penserini, Informatica e Società Digitale - IES, Italy
Stefanos Vrochidis, Centre for Research and Technology Hellas - Thermi-Thessaloniki, Greece
Tsuyoshi Ide, IBM T. J. Watson Research Center, USA
Petr Skobelev, Knowledge Genesis Group / Samara Technical University, Russia
Rajat Mehrotra, Intelligent Automation Inc., USA
Andreas Kercek, Lakeside Labs GmbH, Austria
Claudius Stern, biozoom services GmbH - Kassel | FOM University of Applied Sciences - Essen, Germany

ICAS 2018 Technical Program Committee

Sherif Abdelwahed, Mississippi State University, USA
Lounis Adouane, Institut Pascal (UCA/CNRS/SIGMA), France
Jose Aguilar, Universidad de Los Andes, Venezuela
Alba Amato, Institute for High-Performance Computing and Networking (ICAR), Napoli, Italy
Razvan Andonie, Central Washington University, USA
Richard Anthony, University of Greenwich, UK
Markus Bader, Technische Universität Wien, Austria
Mark J. Balas, Embry-Riddle Aeronautical University, USA
Giovanni Beltrame, Ecole Polytechnique de Montreal, Canada / University of Tübingen, Germany
Julita Bermejo-Alonso, Universidad Politécnica de Madrid (UPM), Spain
Karsten Böhm, Fachhochschule Kufstein, Austria
Radu Calinescu, University of York, UK
Paolo Campegiani, University of Roma Tor Vergata, Italy
Valérie Camps, Paul Sabatier University | IRIT, France
José Manuel Castro Torres, University Fernando Pessoa / LIACC - Artificial Intelligence and Computer Science Laboratory / ISUS - Intelligent Sensing and Ubiquitous Systems, Portugal
Albert M. K. Cheng, University of Houston, USA

Feng Chu, University of Evry, France
Siobhan Clarke, Trinity College Dublin, Ireland
Stéphanie Combettes, University Paul Sabatier of Toulouse, IRIT Lab, France
Prithviraj (Raj) Dasgupta, University of Nebraska, USA
Giovanni De Magistris, IBM Research AI, Tokyo, Japan
Angel P. del Pobil, Jaume I University, Spain
Elisabetta Di Nitto, Politecnico di Milano, Italy
Sotirios Diamantas, University of Nevada, Reno, USA
Akif Durdu, Selcuk University, Turkey
Larbi Esmahi, Athabasca University, Canada
Anna Esposito, Seconda Università di Napoli & IIASS, Italy
Lukas Esterle, Vienna University of Technology, Austria
Thaddeus Eze, University of Chester, UK
Luis Fernando Orleans, Universidade Federal Rural do Rio de Janeiro, Brazil
Hugo Ferreira, INESC TEC / Porto Polytechnic Institute, Portugal
Seyedshams Feyzabadi, Intuitive Surgical Inc., USA
Maurizio Fiasché, Politecnico di Milano, Italy
Manuel Filipe Santos, Universidade do Minho | Research Centre Algoritmi, Portugal
Paolo Fiorini, University of Verona, Italy
Ziny Flikop, Scientist, USA
Stefano Franchi, University of Texas A&M, USA
Matjaz Gams, Jozef Stefan Institute, Slovenia
Fabio Gasparetti, ROMA TRE University, Italy
Marie-Pierre Gleizes, University Paul Sabatier of Toulouse | IRIT, France
Fatemeh Golpayegani, Trinity College Dublin, Ireland
Teodor Lucian Grigorie, University of Craiova, Romania
William Grosky, University of Michigan-Dearborn, USA
Jordi Guitart, Universitat Politècnica de Catalunya (UPC), Spain
Maki K. Habib, The American University in Cairo, Egypt
Fei Han, Colorado School of Mines, USA
Cédric Herpson, University Pierre and Marie Curie (UPMC) | LIP6, Paris, France
Gerold Hoelzl, University of Passau, Germany
Wladyslaw Homenda, Warsaw University of Technology, Poland
Wei-Chiang Hong, Jiangsu Normal University, China
Marc-Philippe Huget, Polytech Annecy-Chambery-LISTIC | University of Savoie, France
Jinho Hwang, IBM T.J. Watson Research Center, USA
Tsuyoshi Ide, IBM T. J. Watson Research Center, USA
Luis Iribarne, University of Almería, Spain
Reza Javanmard, University of Science and Technology of Mazandaran, Iran
Michael Jenkin, York University, Canada
Richard Jiang, Northumbria University, UK
Kevin Jones, University of Plymouth, UK
Paulo Jorge Sequeira Goncalves, Instituto Politecnico de Castelo Branco, Portugal
Imed Kacem, Université de Lorraine, France
Bilal Kartal, University of Minnesota, USA
Alexey M. Kashevnik, St. Petersburg Institute for Informatics and Automation of the Russian Academy of Sciences (SPIIRAS), Russia
Andreas Kercek, Lakeside Labs GmbH, Austria

Won-jong Kim, Texas A&M University, USA
Ah-Lian Kor, Leeds Beckett University, UK
Timo Korthals, Universität Bielefeld, Germany
Igor Kotenko, St. Petersburg Institute for Informatics and Automation of the Russian Academy of Sciences (SPIIRAS), Russia
Satoshi Kurihara, University of Electro-Communications, Japan
Ouiddad Labbani-Igbida, XLIM CNRS UMR 7252 Institute | ENSIL-ENSCI Engineering School | University of Limoges, France
Diego Latella, Consiglio Nazionale delle Ricerche - Istituto di Scienza e Tecnologie dell'informazione "A. Faedo", Pisa, Italy
Jannik Laval, University of Lyon | DISP Lab, France
Jinoh Lee, Istituto Italiano di Tecnologia (IIT), Italy
Alessandro Leone, National Research Council of Italy | Institute for Microelectronics and Microsystems, Lecce, Italy
Noel Lopes, Polytechnic of Guarda, Portugal
Marin Lujak, IMT Lille Douai, France
José Machado, University of Minho, Portugal
Prabhat Mahanti, University of New Brunswick, Canada
Ivano Malavolta, Vrije Universiteit Amsterdam, Netherlands
Jacques Malenfant, UPMC, France
Pushparaj Mani Pathak, Indian Institute of Technology, Roorkee, India
Dinesh Manocha, University of North Carolina at Chapel Hill, USA
Jerusa Marchi, Universidade Federal de Santa Catarina, Brazil
Konrad Andrzej Markowski, Warsaw University of Technology, Poland
Goreti Marreiros, Polytechnic of Porto, Portugal
Rajat Mehrotra, Intelligent Automation Inc., USA
René Meier, Lucerne University of Applied Sciences and Arts, Switzerland
Marcio Mendonça, Universidade Tecnológica Federal do Paraná, Brazil
Yasser F. O. Mohammad, KDDI Laboratories, Japan / Assiut University, Egypt
Masayuki Murata, Osaka University Suita, Japan
Adnan Abou Nabout, Bergische Universität Wuppertal, Germany
Kai Nagel, TU Berlin, Germany
Nicol Naidoo, University of KwaZulu-Natal, South Africa
Vivek Nallur, Trinity College Dublin | University of Dublin, Ireland
Roberto Nardone, University of Naples Federico II, Italy
António J. R. Neves, University of Aveiro, Portugal
Rafael Oliveira Vasconcelos, University Tiradentes (UNIT), Brazil
Flavio Oquendo, IRISA - University of South Brittany, France
Eros Pasero, Politecnico of Turin, Italy / Tongji University, Shanghai, China
Loris Penserini, Informatica e Società Digitale - IES, Italy
Johan Philips, University of Leuven (KU Leuven), Belgium
Francesco Pierri, Universita` degli Studi della Basilicata, Italy
Agostino Poggi, DII - University of Parma, Italy
S.G. Ponnambalam, Monash University Malaysia, Malaysia
José Ragot, Université de Lorraine, France
Sazalinsyah Razali, Universiti Teknikal Malaysia Melaka (UTeM), Malaysia
Douglas Rodrigues, University of Sao Paulo (USP), Brazil
Spandan Roy, Indian Institute of Technology Delhi, India

Copyright Information

Neural Networks for Scattering Signal Based Object Recognition

Hristomir Yordanov and Irina Topalova

Faculty of German Engineering Education and Industrial Management
Technical University of Sofia, Sofia, Bulgaria
Emails: yordanov@fdiba.tu-sofia.bg, itopalova@abv.bg

Abstract—**Radar based imaging techniques can be used to collect 3D information about objects, which in turn can be used to identify and measure specific parameters of these objects. Such measurements need to correlate specific radar signals with the object properties. This can be done using neural networks, as they are designed to search for patterns, which are difficult to find using analytic methods. This work presents a first step towards a neural network based radar signal processing system for object identification by attempting to identify an object placed in a rectangular waveguide.**

Keywords–Scattering signals; Object identification; Neural Networks

I. INTRODUCTION

Radars find many applications as imaging tools. Using the property of electromagnetic waves to partially penetrate and partially reflect from dielectric materials, they can provide 3D images of a large set of objects. The development of easily available high-frequency components up in the microwave, millimetre wave and even THz regions allows for high spatial resolution of the obtained images. This technique finds multiple applications in security systems, the medical systems and in agriculture.

We can consider as an example the sensor described in [1]. The system consists of a 24 GHz Frequency Modulated Continuous Wave (FMCW) radar used to make 3D images of grapevine plants in order to estimate the volume of grapes in a given plant. The radar is equipped with a high gain antenna and is mounted on a pan-tilt platform, which allows for performing azimuthal and elevation scans. The radar bandwidth is 2 GHz. This setup allows for a 7.5 cm depth resolution (that is the precision of the measurement of the distance between the object and the radar) and transverse resolution of 1.5 cm. Of course, using higher signal frequencies and bandwidths and more directive antennas, resolutions in the millimetre range can be achieved [2].

The processing of the radar signal in order to obtain information about the object parameters of interest can be a challenging task. The measurement system described in [1] relies on statistical analysis in order to obtain the grapes volume. Neural networks are optimised for pattern search in complex data. Therefore, they can be used in radar based measurement systems as they can extract the data of interest from the clutter and simultaneously estimate the value of the parameter of interest. In the grapevines radar example, the parameter of interest is the volume of the produced grapes and the clutter is the signals from the plant's trunk and leaves.

In order to develop a full intelligent 3D image processing system, we need to start by implementing simple 1D solutions. In this paper, we present a neural network for shape recognition based on the scattered signal as a benchmark case study.

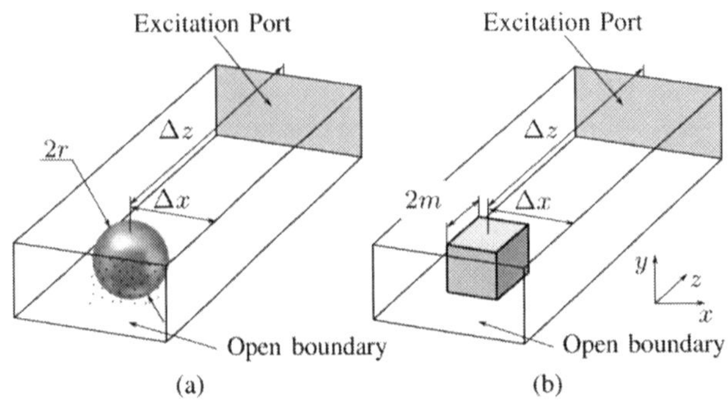

Figure 1. Positioning of a ball of a diameter $2r$ (a) and a cube with edge $2m$ (b) in a WG-12 rectangular waveguide.

The investigated object is an obstacle of perfectly conducting material placed in a rectangular hollow waveguide. This limits the neural network input signal to the spectral representation of a single point reflection signal. The setup has been modelled numerically and the results have been obtained using computer simulation.

Section II describes the setup of the performed simulation and shows the computed reflected signals from the two types of objects in a waveguide. Section III details the neural network based signal processing used to identify the objects based on the reflected signal. Section IV summarises the results and sketches the future work.

II. EXPERIMENTAL SETUP

The experimental setup consists of a hollow rectangular WG12 waveguide with an object placed at distance Δz form the excitation port, as shown in Figure 1. The cross-sectional dimensions of the waveguide are $a = 47.5$ mm and $b = 22.1$ mm. The scattering objects are a sphere of radius r (Figure 1a) and a cube of length $2m$ (Figure 1b). Both objects are made of a perfect electric conductor and are placed at a distance of Δx from the short wall of the conductor. The objects were placed in the middle of the waveguide in the vertical y direction. The excitation port has been placed at the $-z$ end of the waveguide. The opposite end has been terminated with an open boundary in order to model an infinitely extended waveguide and thus eliminate the reflections from that boundary. The model has been simulated for the frequency range of 4 to 6 GHz, which corresponds to the full single mode range of the waveguide. We measure the reflection coefficient at the excitation port. The used simulation tool is CST Microwave studio.

Two families of results have been generated. First, we varied the dimensions of the objects—correspondingly the sphere radius r and the cube edge $2m$—while keeping both

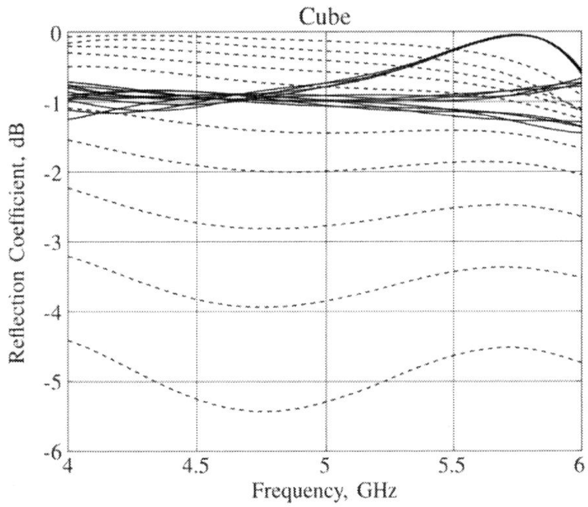

Figure 2. Family of curves showing the magnitude of the reflection coefficient of a waveguide with a conducting cube inside. The solid lines and the dotted lines represent varying position and size of the cube correspondingly.

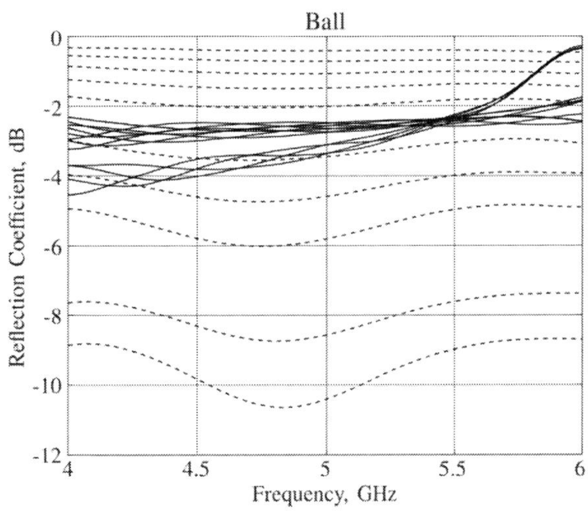

Figure 3. Family of curves showing the magnitude of the reflection coefficient of a waveguide with a spherical object inside. The solid lines and the dotted lines represent varying position and size of the sphere correspondingly.

objects at fixed position $\Delta z = 100\,\text{mm}$ and $\Delta x = a/2$, that is 100 mm from the excitation port and in the middle along the x direction. The size parameters r and m varied from 4 to 10 mm in 0.6 mm steps. Then, we held the object dimensions fixed at $r, m = 7\,\text{mm}$ and varied the offset dimension as follows:

$$\Delta z = 0 \text{ to } -30\,\text{mm in } 10\,\text{mm steps},$$
$$\Delta x = 0 \text{ to } 10\,\text{mm in } 5\,\text{mm steps}.$$

The full combination of offset coefficients has been modelled.

The results for a cube and a ball are presented in Figures 2 and 3, correspondingly, where the dotted lines show the family of curves for varying object size, while the position is held fixed, and the solid lines show the results for fixed size and varying offset. The dotted lines show a greater reflection coefficient ans the object dimensions r and m increase, which can be expected as larger objects create larger echo.

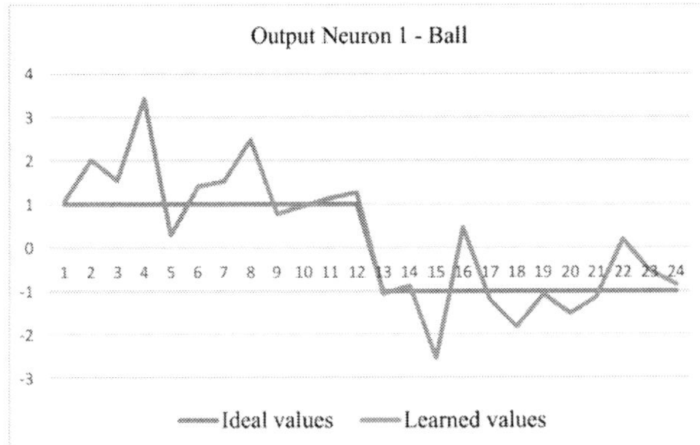

Figure 4. MLP NN (11-8-5-2) output results for Output neuron 1 when recognizing the 12 exemplars of objects *ball* and *cube*.

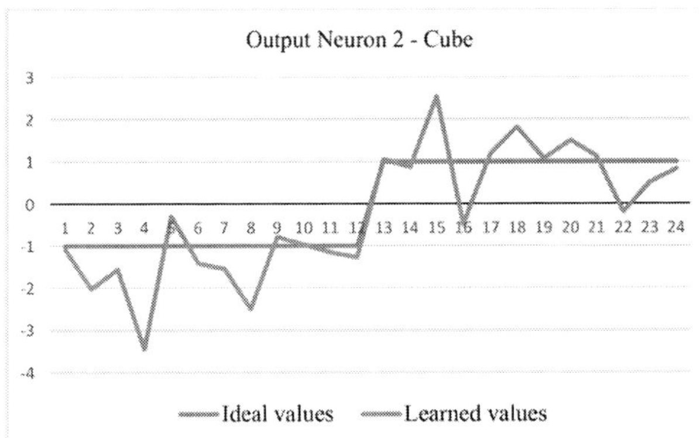

Figure 5. MLP NN (11-8-5-2) output results for Output neuron 2 when recognizing the 12 exemplars of objects *ball* and *cube*.

The frequency distribution of the reflection coefficients have been used to train a neural network to recognise between the two types of objects - a ball and a cube. We have used only 11 points from each curve, as the frequency response varies slowly and using this representation we lose no information. The network has been trained with 10 curves from each object, including curves with varying offset and varying object size, and has been tested with the rest of the curves.

III. Neural Network Signal Processing

As the two 3D objects have similar shapes, it is necessary to use an adaptive and precise method for recognition and classification of the two objects. The Deep Learning method using LP (Multi-Layered-Perceptron) feed forward Neural Network (NN), trained by the BP (Backpropagation) algorithm, gives satisfactory results in these cases [3]. This allows precise placement of boundaries between object classes with overlapping parametric descriptions – in our case very similar reflection signals.

To meet the requirement for fast real-time neural network performance, we need to run small MLP NN structures. Thereafter, the structure may be changed by increasing the number of hidden neurons and /or the number of hidden layers, in order to improve the proportion between response time and the recognition accuracy. The software package NeuroSystem

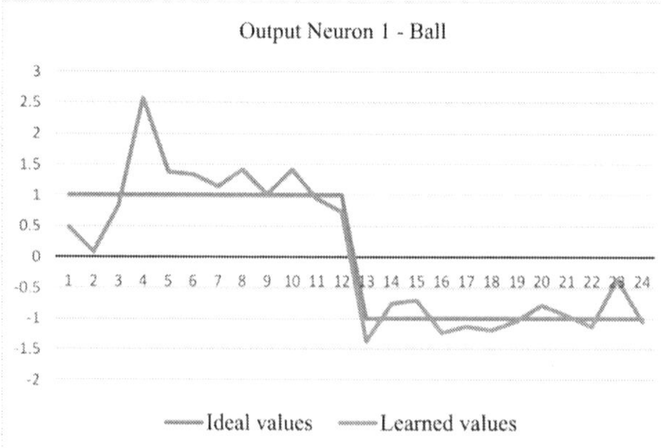

Figure 6. MLP NN (11-10-8-2) output results for Output neuron 1 when recognizing the 12 exemplars of objects *ball* and *cube*.

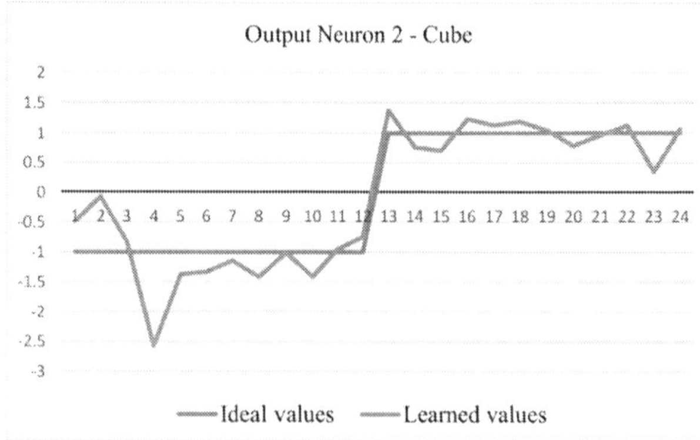

Figure 7. MLP NN (11-10-8-2) output results for Output neuron 2 when recognizing the 12 exemplars of objects *ball* and *cube*.

by Siemens [4] was used for running the experimental simulations.

We have trained the NN with only 11 points from each curve, as they vary slowly in frequency. For each of the two objects, the training set contains 10 curves with varying offset and object size. The test set contains 12 specimens, representing the two types of objects, whose reflected signals have not participated in the training set.

We have designed the NN by adding two hidden layers and increasing the number of neurons in each layer until satisfactory recognition was achieved. The first 100 % recognition accuracy was obtained for object ball when training a 11-8-5-2 MLP NN structure (with two hidden layers, having 8 and 5 neurons and 2 output neurons, representing the two recognizable objects). The MLP NN (11-8-5-2) output results for Output neuron 1 when recognizing the first 12 exemplars of object ball and the second 12 exemplars of object cube are given in Figure 4. The training iterations were stopped when the Mean Square Error (MSE – ε) has reached 5 %. In this case, the obtained recognition accuracy for object cube was 83.3 % (two of twelve tested objects are misrecognized), with results shown in Figure 5. It can be noted that objects 16 and 22 (both are cubes) are incorrectly recognized.

In order to put more precise boundaries between the object classes and to improve the accuracy of recognition, it is necessary to increase the number of neurons in the two hidden layers of the MLP NN. Thus, the next attempt is made with a MLP 11-10-8-2 structure. The training iterations were stopped when the MSE has reached 2 %. In this case the obtained recognition accuracy for both objects was 100 % when tested with the same test set. The obtained results for Output neurons 1 and 2 are given in Figure 6 and Figure 7 respectively. It is good recognizable that the approximation of ideal/ desired values is much better. The summary of the experimental results is shown in Table I.

TABLE I. SUMMARY OF THE EXPERIMENTAL RESULTS.

MLP Structure	Recognition Accuracy, [%]		
	Ball	Cube	MSE – (ε)
11-8-5-2	100 %	83.3 %	5 %
11-10-8-2	100 %	100 %	2 %

IV. CONCLUSIONS AND FUTURE WORK

This paper shows the initial work on identifying suitable neural network signal processing tools for radar based shape recognition techniques. The achieved recognition results show that it is very appropriate to implement MLP NN for 3D object recognition, when using radar reflection signals. The good approximation abilities of the MLP NNs make it possible to recognize even objects of very similar shapes.

As future work, we intend to test the method for a larger number of objects with similar 3D object shapes. Also, to generalize the method, the test sample set will be increased. Additional calculations of approximation error are also foreseen. The presented results provide shape recognition by a single point wideband reflected signal, which is a model of a pulse radar. We intend to expand these results towards scanning pulsed and scanning frequency modulated continuous wave (FMCW) radars.

REFERENCES

[1] D. Henry, H. Aubert, T. Veronese, and E. Serrano, "Remote estimation of intra-parcel grape quantity from three-dimensional imagery technique using ground-based microwave fmcw radar," IEEE Instrumentation Measurement Magazine, vol. 20, no. 3, June 2017, pp. 20–24.

[2] K. B. Cooper *et al.*, "Penetrating 3-d imaging at 4- and 25-m range using a submillimeter-wave radar," IEEE Transactions on Microwave Theory and Techniques, vol. 56, no. 12, Dec 2008, pp. 2771–2778.

[3] J. Schmidhuber, "Deep learning in neural networks: An overview," Neural Networks, vol. 61, 2015, pp. 85 – 117. [Online]. Available: http://www.sciencedirect.com/science/article/pii/S0893608014002135, [retrieved March 2018].

[4] NeuroSystems V4.0 Manuall. Germany: Siemens GmbH, 2016.

Neural Network Based Multimodal Emotion Estimation

A study on Modalities used in Autonomous Systems

Strahil Sokolov
University of Telecommunications and Post
Faculty of Telecommunications, Department of Information Technologies
Sofia, Bulgaria
e-mail: strahil.sokolov@gmail.com

***Abstract*—This paper presents recent research on approaches in autonomous systems for combining multiple modalities for emotion estimation based on neural networks. Emotion recognition is an active area of research especially in the field of autonomous systems in automotive industry, Human Computer Interaction (HCI), multimedia indexing and video surveillance. Both invasive and non-invasive acquisition methods are part of this study. ECG and EEG, Voice and Facial Analysis with modern approaches such as Deep Neural Networks are presented.**

Keywords-deep learning, emotion analysis, multimodal biometrics.

I. INTRODUCTION

Estimating human emotion in Autonomous Systems is an active field of research nowadays. Autonomous Systems in the automotive industry are becoming more and more popular because of the self-driving vehicles. The research in this field enables researchers to seek combination of different biometric modalities through Human-Computer Interface (HCI). HCI is considered the main carrier of human intelligence for the digital world of Autonomous Systems [1]. For the purpose of this research the two main types of acquisition techniques will be considered: invasive and non-invasive. Below are the two modality groups and the respectful modalities which belong to them:

- invasive: EEG, ECG
- non-invasive: face, voice

Invasive HCI depends on the interaction of the following adaptive components: the user generating brain signals with their encoded intent and the interface system translating the signals into instructions to complete the user's intent. The effect of this is that both the user and the sensing autonomous system must have the ability adapt to and complete each other. The encoded user intent in signal features that the interface can measure. The HCI measures these features and translates them into system commands.

In [2] the authors propose a complete end-to-end multimodal emotion estimation system based on voice and facial analysis with deep neural networks. It is proposed to capture the emotional content for various styles of speaking, via robust features. The authors are utilizing convolutional neural network (CNN) to extract features from the speech; the visual modality a deep residual network of 50 layers is used. Then, long short-term memory (LSTM) networks are utilized to make the model more invariant to outliers. The system is trained by taking advantage of the existing correlations of each of the managed streams streams to improve the approach based on auditory and visual handcrafted features for the prediction of spontaneous and natural emotions on the RECOLA database of the AVEC 2016 research challenge on emotion recognition. The reported combined performance for valence is ~0.71 and for arousal ~0.61.

In [3] the authors present a new emoF-BVP database of multimodal (face, body gesture, voice and physiological signals) recordings of actors enacting various expressions of emotions. The database contains audio and video sequences of actors enacting three different intensities of expressions of 23 different emotions along with facial feature tracking, skeletal tracking and the corresponding physiological data. Four deep belief network (DBN) models are proposed and show that these models generate robust multimodal features for emotion classification in an unsupervised manner. The experimental results show that the DBN models are promising for emotion recognition. A convolutional deep belief network (CDBN) models are proposed to learn salient multimodal features of expressions of emotions. The CDBN models have been evaluated on most modern emotion recognition databases and the accuracy reported ranges from 58,5 to 97.3 per cent.

The HCI in this research uses Electroencephalography (EEG) activity or other electrophysiological measures of brain functions as new non-muscular channels for communication and control with smart devices such as wearables. The research aims developing for improvement of autonomous systems in smart mobile applications, based on processing of recorded electrophysiological signals at execution of different mental tasks [7], [8], [9].

Estimation of the basic emotional states is a basic component of intelligent interface of an autonomous systems. The recorded brain signals with experimental setup for two basic emotional states after noise filtering are estimated by clustering and classification using Convolutional Deep Neural Network (DNN), Neural Network (CNN), and statistical features. Classification is performed with Support Vector Machines (SVM). Since the human emotions are modelled as combinations from physiological elements such as arousal, valence, dominance, liking, etc., these quantities are the classifier's outputs. In this research the recorded with experimental setup electrophysiological signals for two emotional states after noise filtering are estimated on the base of clustering and classification with Deep Convolutional Neural Network.

Neural networks have been around for the most part of our era and during the past few years they have been rediscovered. Not only do they solve quite a few computer vision challenges ranging from face recognition to face obfuscation [12] and further to facial emotion recognition as well as challenges in other areas [13].

The authors [14] discuss an approach for emotion recognition "in the wild" based on combination of deep neural networks and Bayesian classifiers. The neural network were used in bottom-up approach, analyzing emotions expressed by isolated faces. The Bayesian classifier estimates a global emotion integrating top-down features obtained through a scene descriptor. According to the validations on dataset released for the Emotion Recognition in the Wild Challenge 2017 the method has been reported to achieve an accuracy of 64.68% on the test set, where the 53.62% was the competition baseline.

The rest of the paper is organized as follows: In Section 2, human emotion model is described. Section 3 presents a proposed schema for EEG acquisition and processing. In Section 4 facial features extraction and processing is presented. At the end of the paper there are the Conclusion and Acknowledgements.

II. TWO-DIMENSIONAL HUMAN EMOTION MODEL

The human emotion is a highly subjective phenomenon: it has been accepted by psychologists that multiple dimensions or scales can be used to categorize emotions. The two–dimensional model of emotion, shown in Figure 1 is introduced in [10]. The valence axis represents the quality of an emotion ranging from unpleasant to pleasant. The arousal axis refers to the quantitative activation level ranging from calm to excited state. This approach for recognition of EEG-based emotions use time and frequency features. The time features are in fact some statistical quantities such as means and standard deviations of the raw signals and its first and second derivatives as well. The classified emotions are: joy, relax, sad and fear.

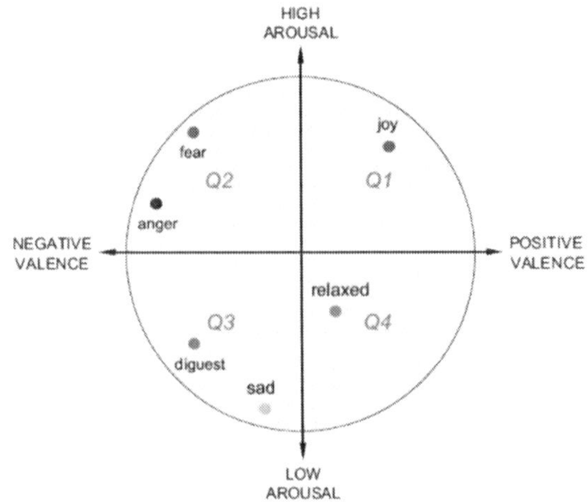

Figure 1: Two–dimensional human emotion model

In [11] the authors use the EEG signal to classify two basic emotions: happiness and sadness. These emotions are evoked by showing subjects pictures. The authors propose a frequency band searching method to choose an optimal band. For this frequency band the recorded EEG signal is filtered. The classification of these two emotions is realized with linear Support Vector Machine (SVM) and Common Spatial Patterns (CSP). Two kinds of trials was used with lengths of $3s$ and $1s$. Classification accuracies on 10 subjects of 93.5% was achieved for 3 s trails and 93% was achieved for $1s$ trials. Their experimental results show that the gamma band ($10Hz$ to 30 Hz) is suitable for EEG-based emotion classification.

Another technique is shown in [10], where the reported accuracy of the emotional valence is about 71%. This technique relies on changes in the power spectrum of short-time stationary oscillatory EEG processes within the standard EEG frequency bands. The features are extracted from very limited set of electrodes and the dimensionality is further reduced with Principal Component Analysis (PCA). The performance is evaluated for arousal, valence and modality separately. With highest classification accuracy over 90% is arousal.

III. EEG PROCESSING AND EMOTION ESTIMATION

The research conducted on EEG preprocessing and Emotion recognition is described in more detail in previous work[15].

For EEG processing the spherical spline method was applied, where the human head is modelled as a sphere. The parameter for spline flexibility is set to its default value of 4. The process of analysis of recorded EEG data is connected with the spectral power of the signal in a set of following standard frequency bands: θ (theta - frequency range from 4 Hz to $7Hz$), α (alpha - 8 Hz to 13 Hz), β (beta-low - 14 Hz to 29 Hz) and γ (gamma - 30 Hz to $45Hz$).

Feature Vectors need to be calculated as follows: for a given EEG channel c and band b a feature vector is composed as follows:

$$\mathbf{f}_{c,b} = [Act_{c,b}, Mob_{c,b}, Cpl_{c,b}] \tag{1}$$

where

$$Act_{c,b} = var\,(j_{c,b}\,(t)) \tag{2}$$

$$Mob_{c,d} = \sqrt{\frac{\mathrm{var}\left(\frac{dj_{c,b}}{dt}\right)}{Act_{c,b}}} \tag{3}$$

$$Cpl_{c,b} = \sqrt{\frac{\mathrm{var}\left(\frac{d^2 j_{c,b}}{dt^2}\right)}{\mathrm{var}\left(\frac{dj_{c,b}}{dt}\right)} - Mob^2_{c,b}}\;. \tag{4}$$

Hjorth parameters, known as activity, mobility and complexity are correspondingly (2), (3) and (4). Arousal estimation the feature vector is organized as augmentation of $\mathbf{f}_{CP6,\theta}$, $\mathbf{f}_{Cz,\alpha}$, $\mathbf{f}_{FC2,\beta}$ and $\frac{Act_{Fz,\beta}}{Act_{Fz,\alpha}}$. Valence estimation is via the feature vector that consists of $\mathbf{f}_{Oz,\theta}$, $\mathbf{f}_{PO4,\alpha}$, $\mathbf{f}_{CP1,\beta}$, $\mathbf{f}_{FC6,\gamma}$, $\mathbf{f}_{Oz,\beta}$, $\mathbf{f}_{Cz,\beta}$, $\mathbf{f}_{T8,\gamma}$ and $\mathbf{f}_{FC6,\gamma}$.

For features selection was chosen the Minimum Redundancy and Maximum Relevance (mRMR) criterion, presented in [15]. The relevance RL of the set of selected features $F = \{f_1, f_2, ..\}$ and target classes C was defined as:

$$RL = \frac{1}{|F|}\sum_{f_i \in F} I(f_i, C) \tag{5}$$

where I denotes the mutual information. The redundancy RD of the features was defined as follows:

$$RD = \frac{1}{|F|^2}\sum_{f_i, f_j \in F} I(f_i, f_j) \tag{6}$$

For incremental search max[$I(F, C)$] is equivalent to max[$RL(F, C) - RD(F)$.]

The features selection from all possible sets is mRMR selection of ratios $\frac{Act_{c,b}}{Act_{k,b}}$, $c \neq k$ and $\frac{Mob_{c,b}}{Mob_{k,b}}$, $c \neq k$ where c and k denote the EEG channel and b is the activity (θ, α or β).

With the acquired EEG signals was formed sequence of Multidimensional Feature Images (FMI). For this purpose the raw EEG signals are measured or extracted from DEAP [8], where for each subject has 40 trails and each trail includes the EEG signals of 32 channels with duration of 60 s. The next step is extraction of power spectrum density as EEG frequency domain feature.

In the current research we join the rapid cascaded classifier with the accurate monolithic one within the two-level combined cascade of classifiers instead of using them independently. This is realized in order to achieve higher detection and lower false alarm rates. The proposed approach for face detection and validation is based on our previous research. It utilizes the OpenCV face detection algorithm [6]. The two-level cascade of classifiers is called "combined" since it combines different types of classifiers: the first level is represented by the Haar-like features' cascade of weak classifiers, which is responsible for the face-like objects detection, and the second level is a CNN for the objects' verification.

For classification was used two different Neural Models. The first is Deep Neural Network comprising of 4 Neural layers. The model contains an initial neural layer of 4000 nodes, followed by layers of 400 and 800 neurons, before the output neural layer of 3 nodes. These nodes are inputs for CNN. All layers are fully connected with Softmax [4] acting as the Activator, and use Dropout [5] technique. The second is a Convolutional Neural Network model designed to classify images effectively. The model uses 2 Convolutional layers.

In this phase the fairly fast face detector is also able to deliver faces in frontal pose. This depends on the training set of images for the CNN. In our approach this has proven to be useful since we are using short-length videos of the subjects' faces may have slight fluctuations off the frontal pose.

The EEG signals were downsampled to 128 Hz, bandpass filtered (4 Hz to 45 Hz). The all data was averaged to the common reference. The performance is validated and evaluated using the k-fold technique. The testing part is extracted from the whole dataset. The rest of the dataset is used to train the classifier. This procedure repeats 20 times and the accuracy is calculated as an average of the accuracies in the iterations.

The Deep Neural Model achieves accuracies for Valence of 73.48% and accuracies for Arousal of 70.35% respectively for classification on high and low classes. For classification on 3 classes - high, normal and low the achieved accuracy is 54.51% for Valence and 51.63% for Arousal.

The Arousal and Valence scores in dataset are given as fractional numbers ranging from 1 to 9. We have quantized these scores to 3, 5 and 7 levels and the testing was performed for each case. The calculated classification accuracies versus dimensionality of the feature vectors is seen on Figure 2.

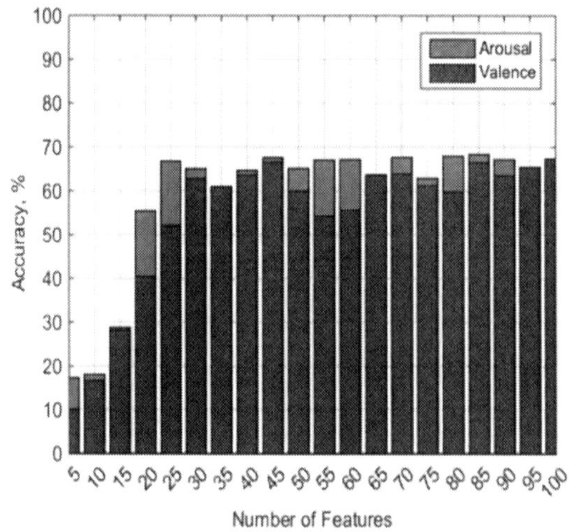

Figure 2: Classification accuracies for arousal and valence versus dimensionality of the feature vectors for CNN

Face emotion estimation runs in parallel and contributes to the improvement of the scores generated by the EEG analysis module. The previously proposed DNN-based face emotion estimation provides an additional improvement for the EEG signal analysis. More experiments need to be conducted on DEAP and other datasets for facial emotion recognition with other DNN structures.

IV. CONCLUSION

An approach for automated multimodal EEG and face-based estimation of human emotions was presented. Estimation of the basic emotional states is a step of building up HCI for disabled persons. The recorded brain signals with experimental setup for two basic emotional states after noise filtering are estimated on the base of clustering and classification with Deep Neural Network, Convolutional Neural Network and statistical features. Classification is performed with support vector machines. Since the human emotions are modelled as combinations from physiological elements such as arousal, valence, dominance, liking, etc., these quantities are the classifier's outputs.

The improvement of the classification is delivered via parallel face emotion analysis system based on DNN. In the ongoing research we are building on top of the achieved framework by experimenting with various Deep Neural Network types and adding other modalities like the ear. The research will be presented in an upcoming study.

REFERENCES

[1] Serbedzija, N. B. "Service components and ensembles: Building blocks for Autonomous Systems." In International Conference on Autonomic and Autonomous Systems (ICAS), Lisbon, Portugal. 2013.

[2] P. Tzirakis, G. Trigeorgis, M. A. Nicolaou, B. W. Schuller and S. Zafeiriou, "End-to-End Multimodal Emotion Recognition Using Deep Neural Networks," in IEEE Journal of Selected Topics in Signal Processing, vol. 11, no. 8, pp. 1301-1309, Dec. 2017.

[3] H. Ranganathan, S. Chakraborty and S. Panchanathan, "Multimodal emotion recognition using deep learning architectures," 2016 IEEE Winter Conference on Applications of Computer Vision (WACV), Lake Placid, NY, 2016, pp. 1-9.

[4] R. A. Dunne, and N. A. Campbell, "On the pairing of the softmax activation and cross-entropy penalty functions and the derivation of the softmax activation function," Proc. 8th Aust. Conf. on the Neural Networks, Melbourne, vol. 185, pp. 181-191, 1997.

[5] N. Srivastava, and R. Salakhutdinov, "Multimodal learning with deep boltzmann machines," Journal of Machine Learning Research, vol. 15, no.1, pp. 2949–2980, 2014.

[6] P. Viola, and M. J. Jones, "Robust real-time face detection." International journal of computer vision," vol. 57, no. 2 pp. 137-154, 2004.

[7] H. Peng, F. Long, and C. Ding, "Feature Selection Based on Mutual Information: Criteria of Max-Dependency, Max-Relevance, and Min-Redundancy," IEEE Transactions on Pattern Analysis and Machine Intelligence, vol. 27, no. 8, pp. 1226–1238, 2005.

[8] S. Koelstra, C. Mühl, M. Soleymani, J.-S. Lee, A. Yazdani, T. Ebrahimi, T. Pun, A. Nijholt, and I. Patras, "DEAP: A Database for Emotion Analysis using Physiological Signals," IEEE Transactions on Affective Computing, vol. 3, no. 1, pp. 18–31, 2012.

[9] X.-W. Wang, D. Nie, and B.-L. Lu, "EEG-Based Emotion Recognition Using Frequency Domain Features and Support Vector Machines," ICONIP'11 Proc. of the 18th int. conf. on Neural Information Processing, part I, pp. 734–743, 2011.

[10] M. Li, and B.-L. Lu, "Emotion classification based on gamma-band EEG," Engineering in Medicine and Biology Society, 2009. Proc. of. The Annual Int. Conf. EMBC pp. 1223–1226, 2009.

[11] P. Lahane and M. Thirugnanam, "A novel approach for analyzing human emotions based on electroencephalography (EEG)," 2017 Innovations in Power and Advanced Computing Technologies (i-PACT), Vellore, 2017, pp. 1-6.

[12] Emeršič Z, V. Štruc P. Peer, "Ear Recognition: More Than a Survey". Neurocomputing. 10.1016/j.neucom.2016.08.139, 2017.

[13] Blaž M, et al. "k-Same-Net: k-Anonymity with Generative Deep Neural Networks for Face Deidentification. Entropy". vol.20. p.60, 2018.

[14] L. Surace et al., "Emotion Recognition in the Wild using Deep Neural Networks and Bayesian Classifiers", sep. 2017.

[15] S Sokolov, Y Velchev, S Radeva, D Radev," Human emotion estimation from EEG and face using statistical features and SVM" Computer Science & Information Technology, pp37-41, 2017

Control of Traffic Congestion with Weighted Random Early Detection and Neural Network Implementation

Irina Topalova
Department of Information Technology
University of Telecommunications and Post, Bulgaria
Sofia, Bulgaria
itopalova@abv.bg

Pavlinka Radoyska
College of Energy and Electronics
Technical University - Sofia
Sofia, Bulgaria
pradoiska@abv.bg

Abstract—**Applying Quality of Service mechanisms to modern communications is essential for the efficiency and for the traffic reliability. The various Quality of Service methods are based on queues management depending on individual traffic parameters. Choosing Quality of Service parameters on the edge network devices defines the management queue and packet discard/queued parameters on the intermediate devices. The proposed research explores the possibility of automatically adapting to the already selected class based Quality of Service policy, of new users added to the backbone of the network. A neural network is trained to automaticlly adapt new end users to the quality of service policy, already set by other end-users and accepted by the intermediate routers. The obtained results show that the automated adaptation of the Quality of Service parameters to the already set ones, is possible for the intermediate routers, and the positive consequences of applying such a method are mentioned.**

Keywords - traffic congestion; Quality of Service; early detection, neural network.

I. Introduction

The aim of Quality of Service (QoS) in communication networks is to guarantee the quality of message delivering by congestion management and congestion avoidance. This is achieved by dividing the traffic in queues and manage any queue individually, based on parameters, configured in any intermediate network device (router or switch). The packets are marked in the endpoint devices, according to the QoS model. Any intermediate device must be configured to create and manage queues, based on this model. Synchronized queue management in all devices is important for quality assurance. The purpose of our work is to find a mechanism by which each new device chooses its configuration parameters for queue management, based on the configuration parameters of the neighboring/end devices. The various QoS methods are based on queues management depending on individual traffic parameters. The chosen QoS parameters on the edge network devices, define the management queue and packet discard/queued parameters on the intermediate devices. The proposed research explores the possibility of automatically adapting to the already selected class based QoS policy, of new users added to the backbone of the network. A Neural Network (NN), defined among many other types of neural networks NNs by Graupe [1] is trained to adapt new end users to the QoS policy, already set by other end-users and accepted by the intermediate routers. The Weighted Random Early Detection (WRED) method, described in Cisco guide [2], was applied to manage and to define the train and test NN parameters. The automatic adaptation of additional networking devices to existing infrastructure with an already-defined QoS policy would lead to the release of human resources and acceleration of the adaptation of traffic parameters in communication management. The experimental results are presented, discussed and a further continuation of the study is proposed.

The rest of this paper is organized as follows. Section II describes the related to the research works. Section III describes and compares differentiated services and weighted random early detection methods. In Section IV, the proposed method for weighted random early detection parameter adjustment is presented. Section V gives the experimental results. The conclusion closes the article.

II. Related Works

The authors Sahu and Sar [3] have created an intelligent method to recognize incoming congestion problems earlier. They train a feedforward neural network with parameters equivalent to the total drop, average per packet drop, cumulative per packet drop, maximum packets drop and minimum packets drop, for send and receive features. The final solution is not automatically obtained as a result of the method, it is left to the administrator. The results are not clear represented and discussed, moreover the authors claim that their developed system missed some points of congestion. Within the model proposed by Calderón, et al. [4], the transmitted packets/traffic were predicted through a neural network, achieving prediction by alternating the input variables (Bandwidth, Congestion Algorithms, QoS, etc.). In this case, in TCP predictions, where one of the most important factors is related to the limitations of this protocol in both the sender and receiver, congestion improvements or methods for QoS were not considered. The different predictions have validity with respect to the real data, obtaining an average error of 4%. The authors Kumar, et al. [5] apply a neural network to predict the actual time needed for transmitting the packet to the destination, depending on the number of hops. As neural network input train parameters, the authors use CWND (Congestion Window) as TCP state variable; Round-Trip Time (RTT) as the length of time it takes for a signal to be sent plus the length of time it takes for an acknowledgement of that signal to be received and the time elapsed from the last loss of a packet. However, this study does not use a method of prioritizing the traffic according to different types of priorities and they do not group traffic into classes according to the priority given by the end routers/ users.

All mentioned researches do not apply more productive/ efficient methods, such as WRED in conjunction with Class-Based Weighted Fair Queueing (CBWFQ), proposed in Cisco guide [2]. They do not interpret the task we offer - to automaticlly adapt new end users to the quality of service policy, already set by other end-users and accepted by the intermediate routers.

III. Differentiated Services and Weighted Random Early Detection

Network congestion occurs when the volume of incoming traffic exceeds the bandwidth of the outgoing channel. Congestion avoidance mechanisms are trying to provoke TCP slow-start algorithm (RFC 2001), implemented in end devices. WRED and differentiated services, implemented in routers, become the most effective approach to prevent the congestions.

A. Active Queue Management congestion avoidance mechanisms

Congestion avoidance in routers is implemented by Active Queue Management (AQM) congestion avoidance mechanisms. Extra packets coming on the inbound interfaces are queued in buffers. The length of the queue is maintained within defined limits by dropping the packets. One of the first effective AQM mechanism is RED (Random Early Detection), proposed by Floyd and Jacobson [6] in the early 1990s. Two critical thresholds for the queue are defined: minimum queue length (***min***q) and maximum queue length (***max***q) and three queue management phases: no drop, random drop, and full drop, shown in Fig. 1. No drop phase is executed only for queue length from 0 to ***min***q. All

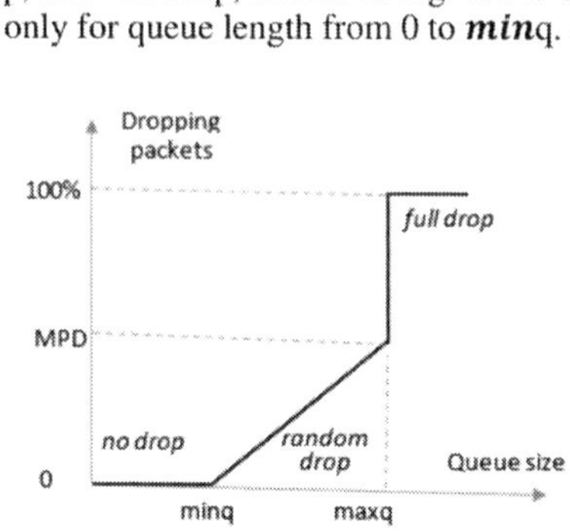

Figure 1. Random Early Detection phases.

packets are buffered. Random drop phase is for queue length from ***min***q to ***max***q. Some packets are dropt. Full drop phase is for queue length above ***max***q. All packets are dropped. The packet drop probability (random drop phase) is calculated based on the average queue length and the MPD (Mark Probability Denominator), Floyd and Jacobson [6]. MPD is the number of dropped packets when the queue size is equal to ***max***q. RED algorithm gives a decision for congestion avoidance problem but has some disadvantages. Firstly, this mechanism does not affect non-TCP protocols. There are risky by insensitive protocols to embezzle the queue. Secondary, the packets from different TCP sessions are not dropped equally and there is a risk of global synchronization problem. Third, the number of dropped packets sharply jump to 100% when the queue size achieves ***max***q size. Different algorithms for the improvement of active queue management are proposed by Abbas et. al. [7]. WRED is a kind of class based queue management algorithms. It uses the same parameters as RED, but it has the ability to perform RED on traffic classes individually. Several traffic classes can be defined within a single queue. Each class has a specific level for the ***min***q, ***max***q and MPD. Packets are classified and joined to a specific class. Drop probability for each packet is calculated according to its class parameters. The packets with lowest ***min***q and/or the highest MPD are dropped preferentially. Every class has the same three phases as the RED algorithm. WRED management queue with three classes: AF1, AF2 and AF3 is presented on Fig.2. AF1 and AF2 have the same ***max***q and MPD parameters. The AF1 ***min***q parameter has the les value then the AF2 ***min***q parameter. Obviously the most packages are dropped from AF1 class, then from AF2 class and finally from AF3 class. The network traffic is divided in several queues to improve fairness in packet dropping. Each queue is managed by the RED, WRED or a similar algorithm. Weighted Fair Queue (WFQ), discussed by Vukadinović and Trajković [8] is a data packet scheduling algorithm. All the queues share outbound bandwidth equally or by predefined ratios. The queues are visited one by one in the cycle period. Every queue sends the amount of packets, according to its share part of the outgoing capacity. The simple WFQ example is presented in Fig.3. Q1 gets 50% of the outgoing capacity, Q2 – 25% and Q3 – 25%. The Scheduler visits Q1 and passes over 2 packets to the output. After that it visits Q2 and passes over 1 packet to the output; visits Q3 and passes over 1 packet to the output, and the cycle is rotated again.

B. Differentiated Services Quality of Service model

There are three main models for providing QoS in a network: Best Effort; Integrated Services (IntServ); Differentiated Services (DiffServ).

DiffServ is called soft QoS model and uses WFQ and WRED algorithms. This model is based on user defined service classes and Per-Hop-Behavior (PHB). The flows are aggregated in traffic classes. The network service policies are defined for each class on any single node. Priorities are marked in each packet using Differentiated Services Code

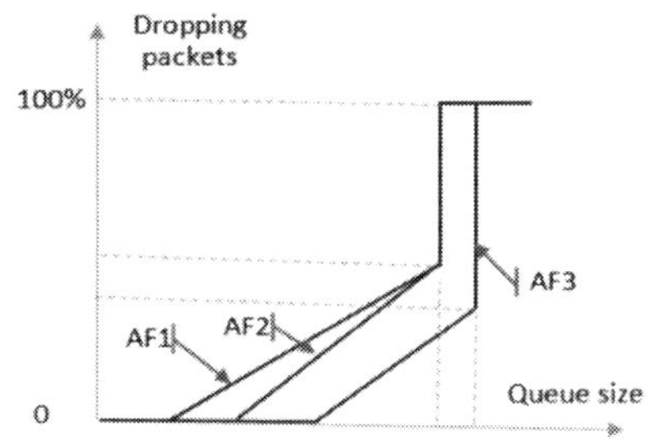

Figure 2. WRED phases.

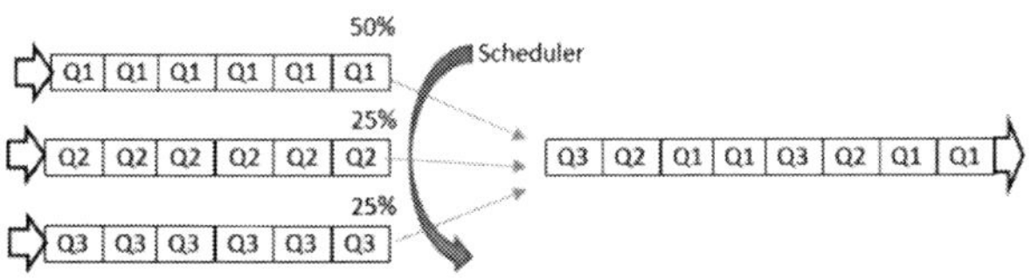

Figure 3. Weighted Fair Queue

Point (DSCP) for traffic classification.

The fields Type of Service (ToS) in IPv4 header (RFC 791) and Traffic Class (TC) in IPv6 header (RFC 2460) are predefined as Differentiated Services Field (DS Field) in RFC 2474. The first six bits of the DS field are used as a code point (DSCP) to select the PHB packet experiences at each node.

DSCP values are described in RFC 2475. They determine the PHB of a packet. Four conventional PHBs are available: two border marks; Class-Selector PHB and Assured Forwarding (AF). DSCP = 000000 marks best effort behavior. All packets with this mark will be dropt when congestion occurs. This is the default PHB. DSCP = 101110 (46 in decimal) marks Expedited Forwarding (EF). EF PHB provides a virtual leased line and is used for critical traffic class as voice traffic. EF PHB provides low-loss, low-latency, low-jitter and assured bandwidth service. DSCP values of "xxx000" ("xxx" are the class selector bits) mark Class-Selector PHB and are used to assure backward compatibility with IP ToS model. DSCP values of "xxxyy0" mark Assured Forwarding (AF) PHB. "xxx" is for user defined AF class and "yy" is for drop precedence of a packet. "01" denotes low drop precedence, "10" – middle and "11" - high drop precedence. AF PHB classes are the subject of this paper.

C. DiffServ model configuration steps

1) Network traffic classification

Performs predominantly on edge for QoS domain router - Cisco Guide [9]. The traffic type is defined by Access Control Lists (ACL) and joined to the specific AF class. Every class is associated with specific DSCP value. Inbound packets are marked with corresponding DSCP value on the edge routers of QoS domain and it is not recommended to change it in the intermediate routers.

2) Queue building

One or more AF classes can be aggregated in one queue, based on PHB parameters. The Queues can be three types: Strict priority queue (LLQ – Low latency queue); Class based queues (managed by WRED algorithm) end best effort queue.

3) Defining queue parameters

The WRED parameters are defined for every queue. For the Strict priority queue is defined guaranteed outbound bandwidth. The rest of outbound bandwidth is distributing between all other queues. For every class based queue is defined:

a) The portion of the bandwidth in percentage;

b) For each AF class (DSCP value) in the queue: min-threshold; max-threshold; MD (Mark-denominator).

Successful congestion avoidance depends on the proper execution of the above three steps. Especially on proper queue management definitions, described in 3) b).

IV. Proposed Method for WRED Parameter Adjustment

In this study, we apply the WRED method for QoS in simple network and use NN to adjust parameters in new added router.

A. Investigated topology

We apply the WRED method for QoS, because it gives relation between AF classes and the most important queue traffic parameters. The topology shown in Fig.4 is considered. It consists of two edge routers (Remotes 1 and 2), an intermediate router(Central) and an edge router "New", which is added later, after the QoS parameters are set in the edge routers. The idea is to train a neural network (NN), implemented in the Central router with WRED parameters: *AF class, min-threshold; max-threshold* and *MD*, according to the IOS command *random-detect*. When an ad-hoc edge router "New" is added with its configured WRED (DSCP) requirements of its network, the already trained NN will approximate/adjust its MD to that already learned by the NN. This adjustment will be performed

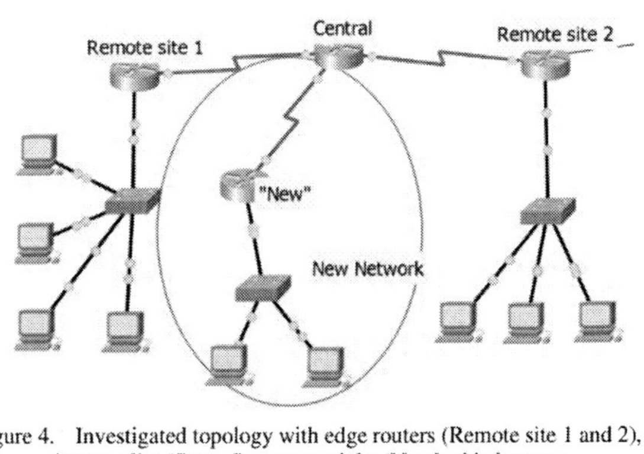

Figure 4. Investigated topology with edge routers (Remote site 1 and 2), intermedite (Central) router and the 'New' added router

automatically without the need for any operator intervention. The new added router will have to comply with the pre-set QoS requirements.

B.Neural Network strategy

To conduct the experiment, we chose a neural network of MLP type, training it with a BP (Backpropagation) algorithm. It was trained with the DSCP values, corresponding to AF Classes 1,2,3 and 4, where Class 1 represents the 'worst queue', for low priority traffic and Class 4 – the 'best queue', for high priority traffic as first parameter. The second and third parameters in the input training set are min-threshold and max-threshold, defined by the command random-detect in the Central router. If the min-threshold is reached, Central router randomly drops some packets with the specified IP precedence. If the *max-threshold* is reached, Central router drops all packets with the specified IP precedence. The MLP has one output neuron and it represents the desired *MD*, where *MD* represents the fraction of packets dropped when the average queue depth is at the *max-threshold*. It means that one out of every *MD* packets will be dropped. Table I represents the correspondence between AF classes, DSCP values and drop precedence. After the NN was trained, a combination of different DSCP values with proposed bandwidth percent for each AF class was provided at its input layer, in order to simulate these parameters, send by the 'New' router. According to the "New" requirements the Central router generates new *min-threshold* and *max-threshold* and forwards the new information to the NN inputs.

TABLE I. AF CLASSES AND CORRESPONDING DSCP VALUES

Assured Forwarding	Low Drop (DSCP)	Medium Drop (DSCP)	High Drop (DSCP)
Class 4	AF41 (34)	AF42 (36)	AF43 (38)
Class 3	AF31 (26)	AF32 (28)	AF33 (30)
Class 2	AF21 (18)	AF22 (20)	AF23 (22)
Class 1	AF11 (10)	AF12 (12)	AF13 (14)

As result the NN gives an output with approximated *MD* value, which is near the value defined initially by the Central. In this way, the 'New' router will be forced to "comply" with the chosen QoS policy.

V. EXPERIMENTAL RESULTS

The initially selected MLP network structure is 6-4-1 and is trained to MSE (Mean-Square-Error) = 0.1. The train data are given in Fig.5. They have 12 input samples as combinations between DSCPs, *min-threshold* and *max-threshold,* defined in Remote 1 and 2. After conducting the test phase with the 'New' data, the obtained *MD* approximation is shown in Fig. 6. The approximation error E_{APROX} is calculated according to (1), where MD_{RSi} is the initial real system value for the Central router, for i-th input

$$E_{APROX} = \sqrt{\sum_{i=1}^{n} \frac{(MD_{RS_i} - MD_{NN_i})^2}{n}} \quad (1)$$

combination, and MD_{NNi} is the NN response, and n is the number of input combinations. In this case EAPROX is 2.56. Obviously, it is necessary to improve the MPL parameters, training a network with improved structure of 6-6-4-1 and with more iterations aiming to reach a smaller MSE. In this case we apply MSE of 0.01. The obtained better results using this NN topology are given in Fig. 7. In this case EAPROX is 0.91. Fig.8 represents the NN 'New' test data with MD approximation. Thus, based on the training of the optimized neural network with the defined AF classes and their initial matching random-detection parameters, we obtain a relatively good MD approximation. Further work is foreseen to test the NN with more combinations of input parameters.

VI. CONCLUSION

In this research, a MLP neural network was trained, aiming to automatically adapt new end users to the quality of service policy, already set by other end-users and accepted by the intermediate routers. The WRED method was applied to manage and to define the train and test NN parameters. The proposed method shows good MD approximation results for the tested input set. The main benefit of the automatic adaptation of additional networking

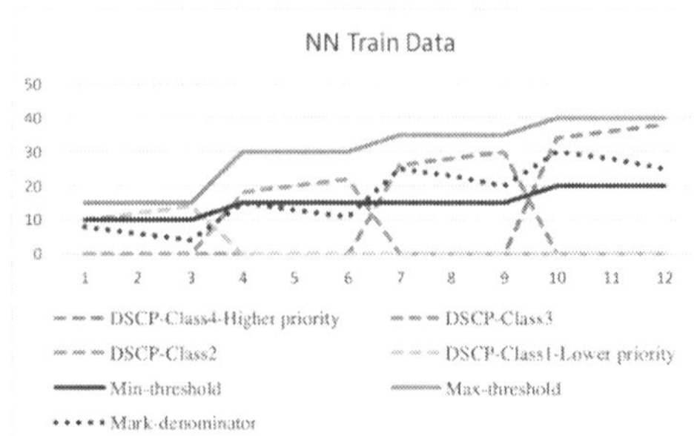

Figure 5. NN train data with initial QoS parameters

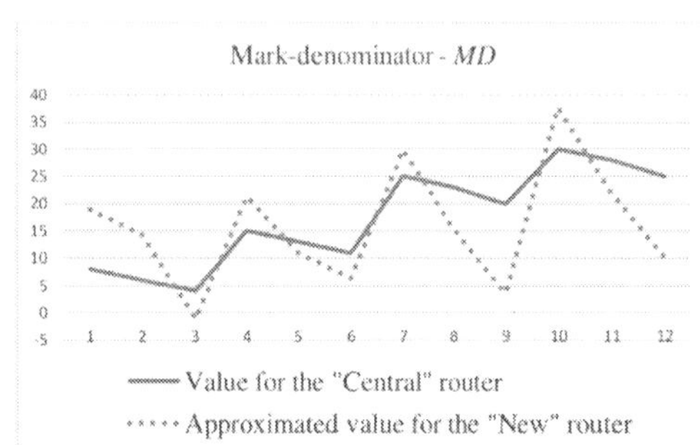

Figure 6. *MD* approximation with MLP – 6-4-1

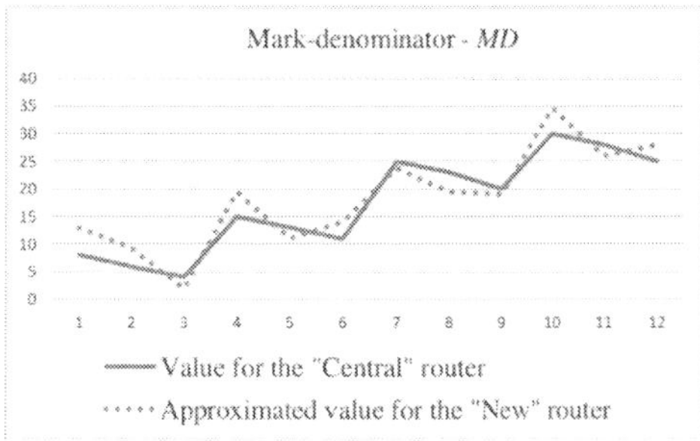

Figure 7. *MD* approximation with MLP – 6-6-4-1

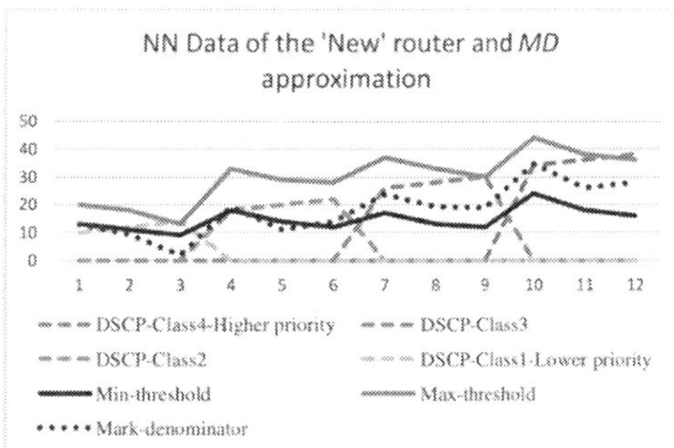

Figure 8. NN 'New' test data with *MD* approximation

devices to existing infrastructure with an already-defined QoS policy, would lead to the release of human qualified resources, needed for manual QoS parameter pre-settings. It also would accelerate the traffic parameters adaptation in communication management and in real time communication. As further work, the input training and test sets may be increased to generalize the method. The idea is to train the NN with the same standard AF classes but with much more possible / reasonable combinations of min-max thresholds, together with a proper proposal for the required link bandwidth at the outputs of the NN. The investigated topology given in Fig. 4, may be tested with more Remote routers and many "New" routers, to test the behavior of the Central router. In this case different NNs could be trained with QoS parameters defined in the different Remotes, and the NN outputs may be combined in input train data for a generalized neural network, to give the final MD proposal. Also software modules will be developed to integrate the neural network into a module of the central router operating system, for direct data exchange between the routers. Aiming to achieve/solve this task, we envisage the use of Python programming language, suitable for implementation in networking operating systems. As hardware devices we intend to use Cisco routers, platforms 2800/2900 with IOS 15.0.

REFERENCES

[1] D. Graupe, 'Deep Learning Neural Networks: Design and Case Studies', World Scientific Publishing Co Inc. pp. 57–110, ISBN 978-981-314-647-1, July, 2016.

[2] https://www.cisco.com/c/en/us/td/docs/ios/120s/feature/guide/fswfq26.html, last accessed 21.04.2018.

[3] Y. Sahu and S. K. Sar, 'Congestion analysis in wireless network using predictive techniques', Research Journal of Computer and Information Technology Sciences, ISSN 2320 – 6527 vol. 5(7), pp. 1-4, September, 2017.

[4] A. F. Luque Calderón, E. J. Vela Porras, O. J. Salcedo Parra, 'Predicting Traffic through Artificial Neural Networks', Contemporary Engineering Sciences, vol. 10, no. 24, pp. 1195 - 1209 HIKARI Ltd, www.m-hikari.com https://doi.org/10.12988/ces. 2017.710146, 2017.

[5] S. S. Kumar, K. Dhaneshwar, K. Garima, G. Neha and S. Ayush, 'Congestion Control in Wired Network for Heterogeneous resources using Neural Network', International Journal of Advanced Research in Computer Science and Software Engineering, Volume 3, Issue 5, May 2013, ISSN: 2277 128X, pp.533-537, 2013.

[6] S. Floyd and V. Jacobson, 'Random Early Detection Gateways for Congestion Avoidance', IEEE/ACM Transactions on Networking, Networking, vol. 1 No. 4, pp. 397-413, August, 1993, Available:http://www.icir.org/floyd/papers/early.twocolumn.pdf

[7] G. Abbas, Z. Halim and Z. H. Abbas, 'Fairness-Driven Queue Management: A Survey and Taxonomy', IEEE Communications Surveys & Tutorials, vol. 18, no. 1, pp. 324-367, Firstquarter 2016. doi: 10.1109/COMST.2015.2463121, 2016.

[8] V. Vukadinović and L. Trajković, 'RED with Dynamic Thresholds for improved fairness', Proceedings of the 2004 ACM symposium on Applied computing (SAC '04). ACM, New York, NY, USA, 371-372. DOI: https://doi.org/10.1145/967900.967980, 2004.

[9] QoS: DiffServ for Quality of Service Overview Configuration Guide, Cisco IOS Release 15M&T, January16, 2013 Available:https://www.cisco.com/c/en/us/td/docs/ios-xml/ios/qos_dfsrv/configuration/15-mt/qos-dfsrv-15-mt-book.html

Defect Inspection of Liquid-Crystal-Display (LCD) Panels in Repetitive Pattern Images Using 2D Fourier Image Reconstruction

Du-Ming Tsai, and Yan-Hsin Tseng
Department of Industrial Engineering and Management
Yuan-Ze University, Taiwan, ROC
e-mail: iedmtsai@saturn.yzu.edu.tw

S. K. Morris Fan
Department of Industrial Engineering and Management
National Taipei University of Technology, Taiwan, ROC
e-mail: morrisfan@mail.ntut.edu.tw

***Abstract*—Flat-panel displays have become increasingly important in recent years for use in handheld devices and video monitors. In this paper, we have considered the problem of detecting micro defects including pinholes, particles and scratches in patterned Thin Film Transistor-Liquid Crystal Display (TFT-LCD) surfaces. The proposed method is based on a global image reconstruction scheme using the Fourier transform. A typical TFT-LCD panel consists of orthogonal gate lines and data lines with TFTs in each intersection of the lines, which result in a structural texture with repetitive patterns. By eliminating the frequency components associated with the structural pattern of data lines, gate lines and TFTs, and back-transforming the Fourier domain image, the reconstructed image can effectively remove the background pattern and distinctly preserve anomalies. A simple adaptive thresholding is then used to segment the defective regions from the uniform background in the filtered image. Experimental results have shown that the proposed method can successively detect and locate various ill-defined defects in a TFT-LCD panel without designing and measuring the quantitative features of individual defect types.**

Keywords-defect detection; automated visual inspection; TFT-LCD; fourier transform

I. INTRODUCTION

Liquid crystal displays (LCDs) using thin film transistor (TFT) arrays are very important display devices used in smart phones, video monitors and televisions. In order to improve the display quality of LCD panels and increase the yield, the inspection of defects in the TFT-LCD panels becomes a critical task in the LCD manufacturing process.

Surface defects of a TFT-LCD panel not only cause visual failure but also cause electrical failure to operate the panel. Appearance defects in a TFT-LCD panel can be roughly classified into two categories: macro and micro defects. Macro defects include "MURA", "SIMI" and "ZURE". MURA means unevenness of color on a TFT-LCD panel. SIMI means stains on a panel, and ZURE means misalignment of a panel. Micro defects include pinholes, particles and scratches (see Figures 7(b1)-(d1) for the sample images). The macro defects appear as high contrast regions with irregular sizes and shapes. They are generally large in size and, therefore, can be detected by human inspectors. However, micro defects are generally very small in size, and cannot be easily found by human personnel or detected with electrical methods. In this paper, we propose a global Fourier reconstruction scheme that especially focuses on the detection of micro defects by utilizing the repetitively structural pattern of TFT-LCD panels.

A. *Related work*

There are several electrical and optical based inspection techniques available for TFT-LCD defect inspection [1]–[3]. The voltage-imaging technique measures the characteristics of a TFT-LCD array by directly measuring the actual voltage distribution on the TFT pixels. The main disadvantage of such approaches is that the probes used for voltage measurement must be separately designed for each panel configuration.

A number of vision-based techniques were developed for LCD defect inspection. Song et al. [4] developed a wavelet-based method to detect the MURA defects in low-resolution LCD images that involve non-textured surfaces. Lu and Tsai [5] applied the Independent Component Analysis (ICA) to detect defects in patterned LCDs. It can effectively detect local defects, but cannot extract the exact shape of a detected defect. Liu et al. [6] also studied the TFT-LCD inspection problem. It used the Locally Linear Embedding (LLE) to extract image features, and then applied the Support Vector Machine (SVM) for classification. The LLE must be carried out in each pixel defined in a small window and is time-consuming to calculate. The SVM requires a training process, and could be sensitive to environment changes. Kim et al. [7] used adaptive multi-level defect detection and probability density estimation for TFT-LCD inspection. It mainly focuses on MURA defects in non-textured surfaces. Lin et al. [8] presented an image processing method for defect detection in TFT-LCD images, where the inspection surface contains only simple data lines and gate lines. The genetic algorithm (GA) heuristic algorithm is applied to adjust the inspection function parameters. Gan and Zhao [9] used the active contour for defect inspection of LCDs. It aims at the MURA defects in non-textured image surfaces of the LCD. The active contour is generally very computationally intensive, and cannot be used for small defect detection in complicated pattern surfaces. Ngo et al. [10] also presented an automatic detection method for MURA defects. The method is based on an accurate reconstruction of the background by training the background from a set of test images. The existing vision-based techniques generally need a pre-stored reference image for comparison. This approach requires precise environmental controls such as alignment and lighting for the TFT-LCD panel under inspection. In our previous work [11], we proposed a Fourier-based method for defect detection in directional textures. It works successively for the LCD panels in a low resolution image that shows no TFT patterns. It fails to detect small defects in the LCD surfaces that present data lines, gate lines and TFTs.

B. Overview of the proposed method

In the LCD manufacturing process, perpendicular data and gate conductive lines are patterned onto the glass substrate. A thin film transistor is located at each intersection of the data and gate lines. Figure 1 demonstrates the magnified image of a TFT-LCD panel under the resolution of 120 pixels/mm. It comprises repetitive, horizontal gate lines and vertical data lines, in which the small black rectangular component at each intersection of lines is the TFT. Since the geometrical structure of a TFT-LCD panel surface involves repetitive, equally-spaced horizontal and vertical lines, it can be classified as a structural texture with oriented line pattern. The structural pattern of a TFT-LCD panel results in a homogeneously textured image that consists of an arrangement primarily of horizontal and vertical lines appearing periodically on the surface. The problem of defect detection in TFT-LCD panel surfaces can now be considered as a texture analysis problem in image processing.

The proposed method does not rely on conventional methods of textural feature extraction. It is based on a global image reconstruction scheme using the Fourier transform. The Fourier spectrum is ideally suited for describing the directionality of periodical line patterns in an image. The proposed Fourier-based image reconstruction scheme fully utilizes the structural characteristics of TFT-LCD panels by setting the frequency components that are associated with the repetitive, orthogonal lines and TFTs of a TFT-LCD panel image to zero, and back-transforming the Fourier domain image. The Fourier reconstruction process will then remove all background texture of the TFT-LCD panel surface, and distinctly preserve local anomalies in the filtered image. This converts the difficult defect detection in a complicated textured-image to a simple thresholding in a uniform image. The statistical process control is then used to set up the control limits (i.e., thresholds) for distinguishing between defective regions and faultless regions in the reconstructed image.

This paper is organized as follows: Section II first discusses the Fourier transform and the properties of repetitive TFT-LCD pattern in the Fourier plane. The removal of repetitive line and TFT patterns in the TFT-LCD panel is then described. Section III presents the experimental results from a number of TFT-LCD panel surfaces that contain faultless regions and micro-defects of pinholes, particles and scratches. The paper is concluded in Section IV.

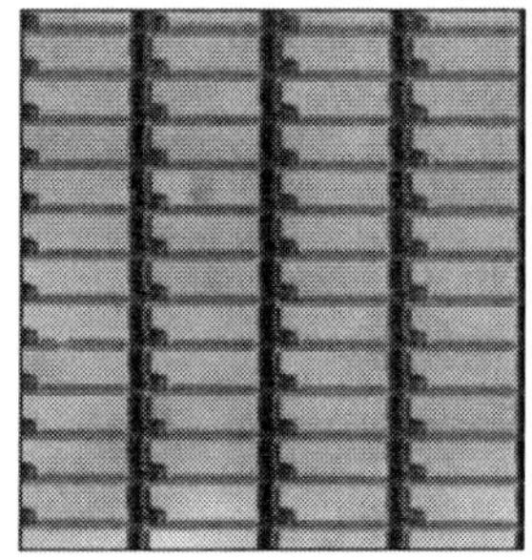

Figure 1. The image of a TFT-LCD panel under the fine resolution of 120 pixels/mm.

II. FOURIER IMAGE RECONSTRUCTION

In this paper, we use machine vision to solve the problem of defect detection in TFT-LCD panels. The Fourier-based image reconstruction technique is used to remove repetitively structural patterns in TFT-LCD surfaces.

Let $f(x, y)$ be the gray level at coordinates (x, y) in the spatial domain image of size $N \times N$. The discrete two-dimensional Fourier transform of $f(x, y)$ is given by

$$F(u,v) = \sum_x \sum_y f(x,y) \cdot \exp[-j2\pi(ux+vy)/N] \tag{1}$$

for frequency variables $u, v = 0,1,2,...,N-1$. The spectrum $F(u,v)$ is then centered. The Fourier transform is generally complex. That is, $F(u,v) = R(u,v) + jI(u,v)$, where $R(u,v)$ and $I(u,v)$ are the real and imaginary parts of $f(x,y)$, i.e.

$$R(u,v) = \sum_x \sum_y f(x,y) \cdot \cos[2\pi(ux+vy)/N] \tag{2}$$

$$I(u,v) = \sum_x \sum_y f(x,y) \cdot \sin[2\pi(ux+vy)/N] \tag{3}$$

The power spectrum $P(u,v)$ of $F(x,y)$ is defined by

$$P(u,v) = |F(u,v)|^2 = R^2(u,v) + I^2(u,v) \quad (4)$$

A. Removal of data and gate lines

A typical TFT-LCD panel consists of horizontal gate lines on one plane, and vertical data lines on the other plane. It results in an image of structural texture that contains orthogonal lines. Figures 2(a) and 3(a) show two TFT-LCD sample images: one is a faultless surface, and the other contains a pinhole defect. Figures 2(b) and 3(b) present the power spectra of the respective TFT-LCD surface images as an intensity function, where the brightness is proportional to the magnitude of the power spectrum $P(u,v)$. Note that the transform of periodical data and gate lines in the spatial domain image results in high-energy frequency components distributed along the horizontal and vertical lines passing through the center in the Fourier plane. Compared to the Fourier spectrum of the associated faultless TFT-LCD sample image, Figure 3(b) reveals that the pinhole defect has significant contribution to the frequency components around the center of the Fourier plane.

In order to remove the orthogonal data and gate lines in a TFT-LCD surface image, we can edit the Fourier domain image and set the associated high-energy frequency components to zero, and then apply the inverse Fourier transform to reconstruct the image. Let Δw denote by the notch width that determines the neighborhood regions for high-energy frequency components along both the horizontal line and vertical line in the Fourier plane. The high-energy frequency components associated with the orthogonal data and gate lines in the TFT-LCD plane are set to zero as follows:

Delete the frequency components within the horizontal notch of width Δw, i.e.

$$F(u,v) = 0 \text{ for all u's, and } v = 0, \pm 1, \pm 2, \ldots, \pm [\Delta w / 2]$$

so that the repetitive data lines in the spatial domain image can be removed. Also, delete the frequency components within the vertical notch of width Δw, i.e.

$$F(u,v) = 0 \text{ for all } v\text{'s, and } u = 0, \pm 1, \pm 2, \ldots, \pm [\Delta w/2]$$

so that the repetitive gate lines can be removed. With the newly assigned values of $F(u,v)$, the reconstructed image can be obtained using the discrete inverse Fourier transform. That is

$$\hat{f}(x,y) = \frac{1}{N^2} \sum_u \sum_v F(u,v) \cdot \exp[j2\pi(ux+vy)/N] \quad (5)$$

Figures 2(c) and 3(c) present, respectively, the reconstructed images of Figures 2(a) and 3(a) using the notch width Δw of 1 pixel, i.e., $F(u,0) = 0$ and $F(0,v) = 0$ for all u's and v's. The results show that the orthogonal data and gate lines in both faultless and defective TFT-LCD sample images are basically removed, and the pinhole defect is well preserved in the filter image. However, residuals distributed periodically along the vertical direction remain in both reconstructed images of the faultless and the defective TFT-LCD panel surfaces. The residuals in the filtered image are the result of the patterned TFTs that locate at each intersection of the data and gate lines.

B. Removal of TFTs

Given the Fourier spectrum of any complicated gray-level image, the frequency components circularly around the center of the Fourier plane are low frequency bands that represent the coarse approximation of the original gray-level image, and those apart from the center are high frequency bands that represent the details of the original image. As seen in Figure 3(b), the local anomaly embedded in a homogeneous texture contributes the frequency components around the center of the Fourier plane. The details of the homogeneous background texture are spread in the high frequency zone in the Fourier plane.

By applying the band reject filtering that deletes all frequency components outside the circle of a specific radius, the details of TFTs in the original gray-level image can be removed. As the filter radius increases, more details will be preserved in the reconstructed image. We can sufficiently remove all background texture of TFT-LCD panels and distinctly preserve anomalies in the filtered image by simultaneously deleting all frequency components on the horizontal and vertical lines passing through the center and those outside the circle of a given radius r^* in the Fourier plane, i.e.

$F(u,0) = 0, \forall u$; $F(0,v) = 0, \forall v$; and

$$F(u,v) = 0 \text{ for all } (u^2 + v^2)^{1/2} > r^* \quad (6)$$

The discrete inverse Fourier transform in eq. (5) is then applied to reconstruct the image.

Figures 4(b) and 5(b) show the Fourier spectra of the two TFT-LCD test samples in Figures 2(a) an 3(a), in which the black regions represent the frequency components with a set value of zero, i.e., $F(u,v)=0$. The selected filter radius r^* for TFT removal is 30 pixels for both test samples. The results in Figures 4(c) and 5(c) show that the reconstructed image of the faultless TFT-LCD panel surface in Figure 2(a) becomes a uniform white image, and that of the defective surface in Figure 3(a) contains only the pinhole defect.

Finally, we use the simple statistical process control limit to set up the threshold for distinguishing defects from the uniform background in the reconstructed image. The upper and lower control limits for intensity variation in the filtered image are given by $\mu_{\hat{f}} \pm K\sigma_{\hat{f}}$, where $\mu_{\hat{f}}$ and $\sigma_{\hat{f}}$ are the mean and standard deviation of gray values in the whole reconstructed image. K is a control constant, which is generally in the range between 2 and 5.

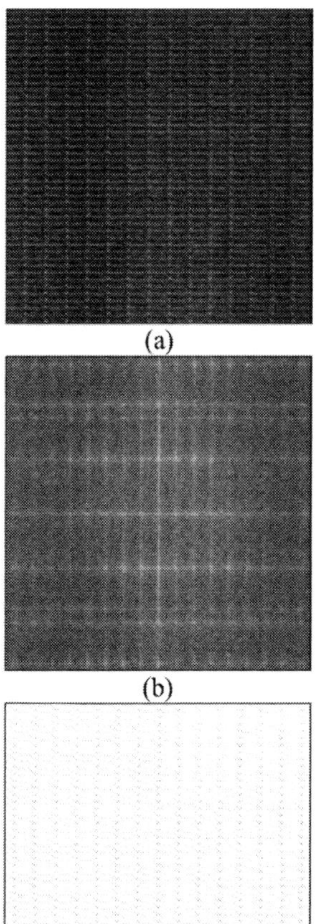

Figure 2. (a) A faultless TFT-LCD surface; (b) the corresponding Fourier power spectrum; (c) the reconstructed image by setting $F(u,0)=0$ and $F(0,v)=0$.

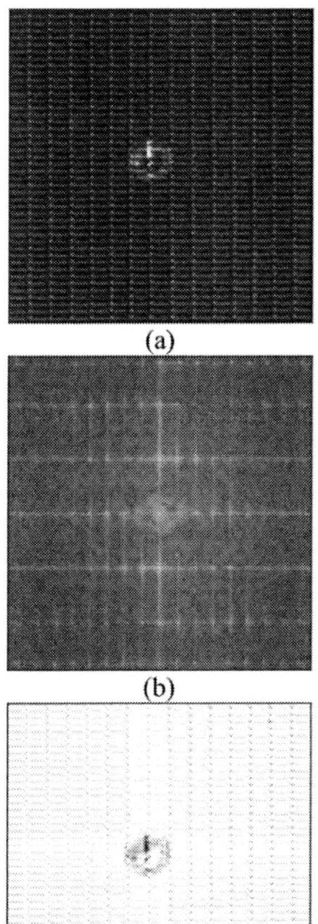

Figure 3. (a) A defective TFT-LCD surface with a pinhole; (b) the corresponding Fourier power spectrum; (c) the reconstructed image by setting $F(u,0)=0$ and $F(0,v)=0$.

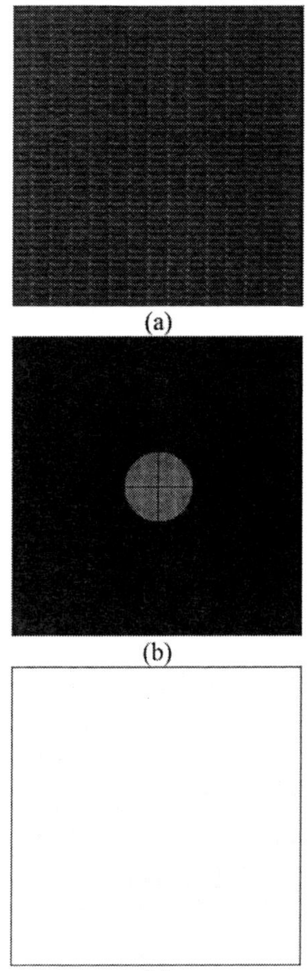

Figure 4. (a) The same faultless TFT- LCD sample shown in Figure 2(a); (b) the corresponding power spectrum, in which the black regions represent $F(u,v)$ with a set value of zero; (c) the reconstructed image from (b).

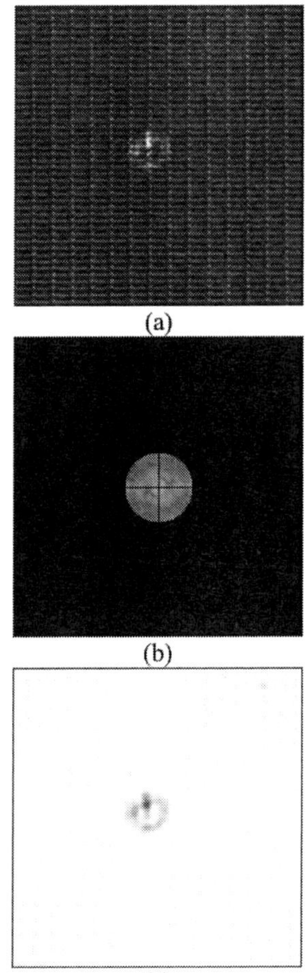

Figure 5. (a) The same defective TFT- LCD sample shown in Figure 3(a); (b) the corresponding power spectrum, in which the black regions represent $F(u,v)$ with a set value of zero; (c) the reconstructed image from (b).

III. EXPERIMENTS AND DISCUSSION

In this section, we present experimental results from a variety of micro defects including pinholes, particles and scratches in TFT-LCD panel surfaces to evaluate the efficacy of the proposed Fourier reconstruction scheme. Figure 6 shows the schema of the proposed automated visual inspection system, and the scan trajectory of the camera of a large LCD panel. The camera and light source are straightly on the top of the TFT-LCD panel. Two green bar-shaped LED lights are used for the illumination. The proposed Fourier-based method is fast enough to process the inspection while the camera is moving around the LCD panel. The test images are 256×256 pixels wide with 8-bit gray levels. Figure 7(a1)-(d1) shows respectively four images that involve a faultless surface, and three defective surfaces of pinhole, particle and scratch under the image resolution of 60 pixels/mm. These three micro defects can only be detected in images of a fine resolution, and cannot be reliably observed in images with a resolution below 50 pixels/mm.

The proposed method does not require defect-free TFT-LCD images for reference, and is tolerable to environmental changes, such as shifting and lighting. The notch width Δw used for eliminating the frequency components associated with orthogonal data and gate lines is 1 pixel for all test images. Throughout a preliminary experiment, a radius r^* of 30 pixels is used for all test samples in the detection of pinholes, particles and scratches. A large control constant $\mathcal{K}$ of 5 is used in this study for the final segmentation in the reconstructed image.

Figures 7(a2) through (d2) show the reconstructed results of the four test images in Figure 7(a1)-(d1), respectively. Figures 7(a3)-(d3) present the defect detection results of the reconstructed images, where pixels with gray values falling outside the control limits are marked in black, and the ones falling within the control limits appear in white. The results reveal that the resulting image of the faultless TFT-LCD surface is uniformly white, and the defects in all three defective surfaces are correctly segmented in the binary images. The suspect defects (i.e., the black points in the binary image) are further classified by evaluating the sizes (for particles and pinholes) and lengths (for scratches, using the Hough transform to accumulate the pixels on a line) in the binary image. An additional experiment that involves 100 defect-free test samples and 63 defective test samples is also conducted. The experimental results show all defective samples including particles, pinholes and scratches can be identified without false alarms if the defect sizes are larger than 5×5 pixels. The proposed method can detect a defect as small as 0.17 mm in physical size. The processing time of Fourier transform and inverse Fourier transform is around 0.1 seconds for an image of size 256×256 on a typical personal computer.

IV. CONCLUSIONS

In this paper, we have considered the problem of detecting micro defects embedded in TFT-LCD patterned surfaces. The proposed method is based on a global image reconstruction scheme using the Fourier transform. The merit of the proposed method is that it can be used to detect various ill-defined defects in a TFT-LCD panel without designing and measuring the quantitative features of individual defect types, and requires no template for the comparison.

The method proposed in this paper can be considered as a supervised one since the proper notch width Δw and filter radius r^* must be predetermined. It can be selected according to the structural pattern of a TFT-LCD panel under a given image resolution. The proposed method in this study mainly focuses on the detection of micro defects. It can be extended to the inspection of non-structured anomalies, such as MURA, or fingerprint in a low-resolution image of the patterned TFT-LCD panel.

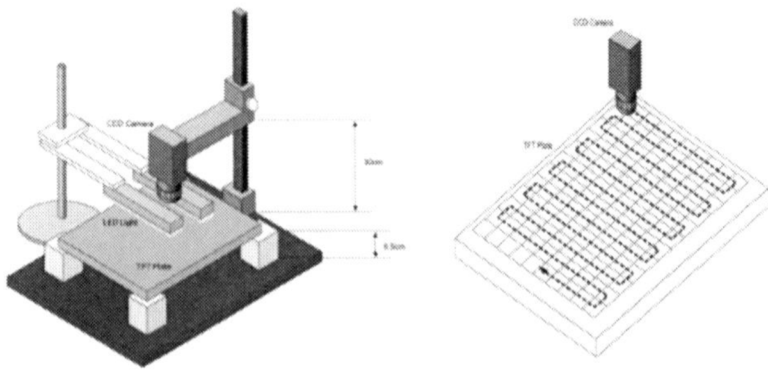

Figure 6. The configuration of the automated LCD inspection system, and the scan trajectory of the camera.

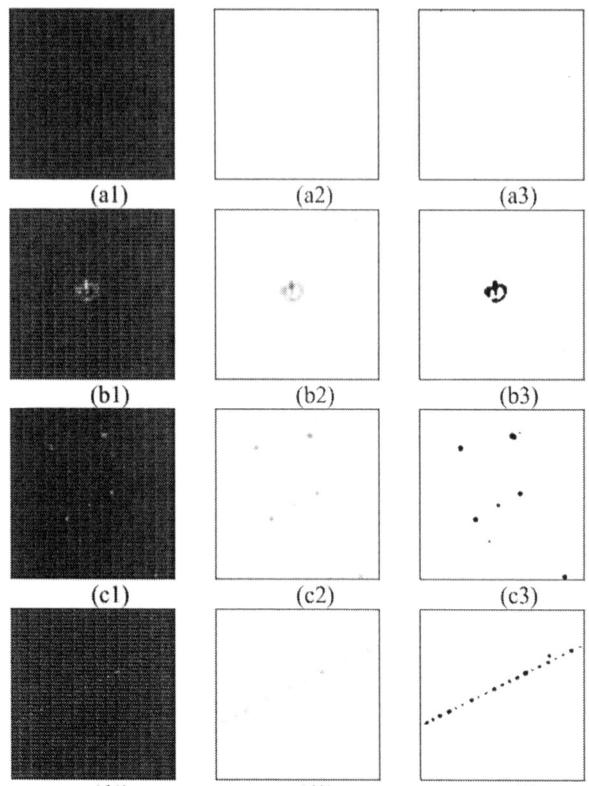

Figure 7. Four TFT-LCD panel images used for test: (a1) a faultless TFT-LCD surface; (b1)-(d1) defective TFT-LCD surfaces with respective pinhole, particle and scratch defects; (a2)-(d2) reconstructed images; (a3)-(d3) resulting binary images.

REFERENCES

[1] P. O Chen, S. H. Chen and F. C. Su, "An effective method for evaluating the image- sticking effect of TFT-LCDs by interpretative modeling of optical measurement," *Liquid Crystals*, vol. 27, 2000, pp. 965-975.

[2] J. Hawthorne, "Electro-optics technology tests flat-panel displays," *Laser Focus World*, vol. 36, 2000, pp. 271-276.

[3] C. S. Lin, W. Z. Wu, T. L. Lay and M. W. Chang, "A digital image-based measurement system for a LCD backlight module," *Optics and Laser Technology*, vol. 33, 2001, pp. 499-505.

[4] Y. –C. Song, D.-H. Choi and K.-H. Park, "Wavelet-based image enhancement for defect detection in thin film transistor liquid crystal display panel," *Japanese Journal of Applied Physics*, vol. 45, 2006, pp. 5069-5072.

[5] C.-J. Lu and D.-M. Tsai, "Independent component analysis-based defect detection in patterned liquid crystal display surfaces," *Image and Vision Computing*, , vol. 26, 2008, pp. 955-970.

[6] Y.-H. Liu, Y.-K. Huang and M.-J. Lee, "Automatic inline defect detection for a thin film transistor-liquid crystal display array process using locally linear embedding and support vector data description," *Measurement Science and Technology*, vol. 19, 2008, 095501.

[7] S.-Y. Kim, Y.-C. Song, C.-D. Jung and K.-H. Park, "Effective defect detection in thin film transistor liquid crystal display images using adaptive multi-level defect detection and probability density function," *Optical Review*, vol. 18, 2011, pp. 191-196.

[8] C.-S. Lin, Y.-C. Liao, Y.-Long Lay, K.-C. Lee and M.-S. Yeh, "High-speed TFT LCD defect-detection system with genetic algorithm," *Assembly Automation*, vol. 28, 2008, pp. 69-76.

[9] Y. Gan and Q. Zhao, "An effective defect inspection method for LCD using active contour model," *IEEE Trans. on Instrumentation and Measurement*, vol. 62, 2013, pp. 2438-2445.

[10] C. Ngo, Y.-J. Park, J. Jung, R.-U. Hassan and J. Seok, "A new algorithm on the automatic TFT - LCD mura defects inspection based on an effective background reconstruction", *Journal of Society for Information Display*, vol. 25, 2017, pp. 737-75.

[11] D.-M. Tsai and C.-Y. Hsieh, "Automated surface inspection for directional textures", *Image and Vision Computing*, vol. 18, 1999, pp. 49-62.

Key Parameter Identification for Faulty Wafer Detection Using Image Processing

Shu-Kai S. Fan[1], Du-Ming Tsai[2], Chih-Hung Jen[3], Rui-Yu Huang[1] and Kuan-Lung Chen[1]

[1]Department of Industrial Engineering and Management
National Taipei University of Technology, Taiwan, ROC
Email: morrisfan@ntut.edu.tw, ray4733430@yahoo.com.tw, ms199323@gmail.com

[2]Department of Industrial Engineering and Management
Yuan-Ze University, Taiwan, ROC
Email: iedmtsai@saturn.yzu.edu.tw

[3]Department of Information Management
Lunghwa University of Science and Technology, Taiwan ROC
Email: f7815@mail.lhu.edu.tw

***Abstract*—Nowadays, the semiconductor industry has become fully automated during the manufacturing process where abundant process parameters are collected on-line by sensor for the Fault Detection and Classification (FDC) purpose. To analyze these parameters and identify a smaller set of key parameters that have crucial influence on wafer quality must bring great benefits in stabling the manufacturing process and enhancing the production yield. Therefore, this article considers an alternative approach to use image processing techniques for analyzing the raw trace data. First, the one-dimensional time series data of a wafer batch was transformed into a two-dimensional image. Fisher's Criterion (FC) ratios of the labelled good and defect wafer images are computed. The parameters that have high FC ratios are deemed the key parameters. The nine key parameters were identified by using the proposed image processing technique, which concurs with the technical experiences from the process engineers.**

KeyWords*: *Semiconductor manufacturing, Key parameter identification, Image Processing, Fisher's criterion

I. Introduction and Proposed Method

Nowadays, in the semiconductor manufacturing practice, wafer manufacturing is a complicated multiple-step sequence of photolithographic and chemical processing steps during which electronic circuits are gradually fabricated on a wafer made of pure semiconducting material; that is, the so-called "raw trace data." Likewise, a gigantic amount of data with a wide variety of process parameters are simultaneously generated. Raw trace data are automatically recorded in every sensor during manufacture processes, so multiple time series data are produced wafer by wafer. The final wafer quality should be, in essence, highly related to some key parameters. In ordinary practice, the engineers use their practical experiences gained from extensive experimental results and historical testing data to decide on potential key parameter. Therefore, the investigation of possible key parameters among the raw trace data poses a challenging task for process engineers in semiconductor manufacturing.

To improve the production yield and maintain the process stability, identifying the key parameters from the raw trace data is an important issue in routine manufacturing. Feature selection aims to downsize the amount of the raw trace data but still maintains the key information. In the Advanced Process Control (APC) practice, the raw trace data are collected by sensor continuously. The process control engineer will use this kind of data to perform the Fault Detection and Classification (FDC) and process control/monitoring tasks. Traditional FDC approaches in semiconductor manufacturing use univariate statistics for monitoring, which is tedious and might be misleading if key parameters cannot be correctly identified. Although the APC of semiconductor manufacturing has advanced considerably in the past decade, this paper attempts to propose an alternative approach by means of image processing techniques to analyze the raw trace data for identifying key parameters.

In the open literature, there exist many researches that transform a two-dimensional image data into one-dimensional data and apply traditional statistical methods for post hoc analysis. For instance, Bartlett et al. [1] proposed using Independent Component Analysis (ICA) to study face recognition. On the contrary, from a reverse point of view, the one-dimensional raw trace data collected for this article will be recast into a two-dimensional image, and then existing image processing methods can be readily employed.

A semiconductor manufacturing process that consists of 38 parameters in the raw trace data set was under investigation. In the data set, there are 155 wafers monitored, labelled with 134 good and 21 defect wafers. For each parameter, the 155×180 measurements of 155 wafers and 180 readings are placed in an image as shown in Figure 1.

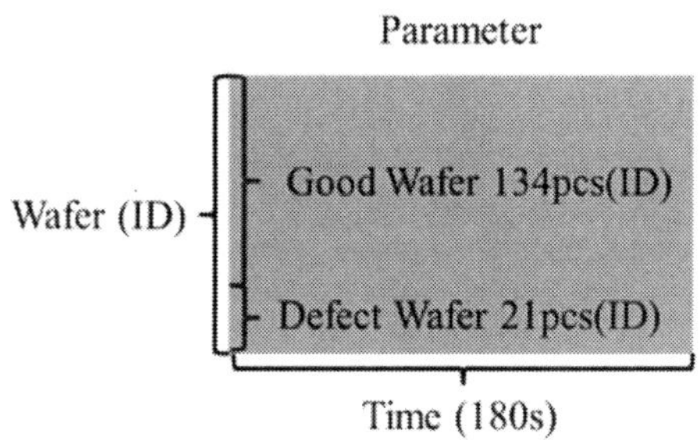

Figure1. Parameter Image.

These 38 parameters are BufPurge N2 MFC Flow, Buffer Chamber Robot Correct EXT, Buffer Chamber Robot Correct ROT, CHILLED WATE R TEMP, CH Inner Heater Zone Temp, CH Outer Heater Voltage Ratio Mode, Chamber heater pid error, H2_Flow Setpoint1, H2_MFCFlow, Heater servo fwd, N2 Flow Setpoint1, N2 MFC Flow, N2 PURGE Flow Setpoint1, N2 PURGE_MFC Flow, NF3_MFCFlow, Number Wafer In Periodic Clean Process, PH3 Flow Setpoint1, PH3 MFC Flow, SiH4 Flow Setpoint1, SiH4 MFC Flow, Temperature Power, Chamber fore line pressure, Chamber heater lift spacing, Chamber heater lift step number, Chamber inner heater zone current, Chamber inner heater zone power, Chamber inner heater zone resistance, Chamber inner heater zone voltage, Chamber lift position, Chamber misc number of wafer count, Chamber outer heater current, Chamber outer heater power, Chamber outer heater resistance, Chamber outer heater voltage, Chamber pm current wafer count, Chamber pressure reading, Chamber recipe elapsed time, and Chamber throttle valve position.

In this study, the raw trace data was transformed into an 8-bit gray-level representation. The maximum value is 255, so the grey level range would be from 0 to 255. The minimum value 0 represents black and the maximum value 255 represents white.

For each wafer, a univariate statistic, the Signal-to-Noise Ratio (SNR) is calculated as in (1).

$$SNR = \frac{\mu}{\sigma} \qquad (1)$$

In (1), μ is the mean and σ is the standard deviation. Under a particular parameter, the SNR is evaluated wafer-wise, generating a transformation from a time series realization into the feature of wafer's parameter. From a practical viewpoint, a key parameter must be able to clearly differentiate between good and defective wafers. Therefore, it is highly anticipated that the SNR of good wafers exhibits an obvious difference as compared to that of defective wafers.

Next, Fisher's criterion (FC) ratio is used to identify the key parameters from the 38 parameters. As usual, FC tries to find a projection direction, attempting to increase the separation between classes while minimizing the variance within a class [2][3] (see Figure 3). In the paper, the SNR is used to compute each parameter's FC ratio wafer by wafer. Firstly, the SNRs are classified into two categories: good and defective in that labelling was previously done. The good wafers fall into group 1 and the defective wafers fall into group 2. Since there are 38 parameters in total, there are 38 FC ratios as well.

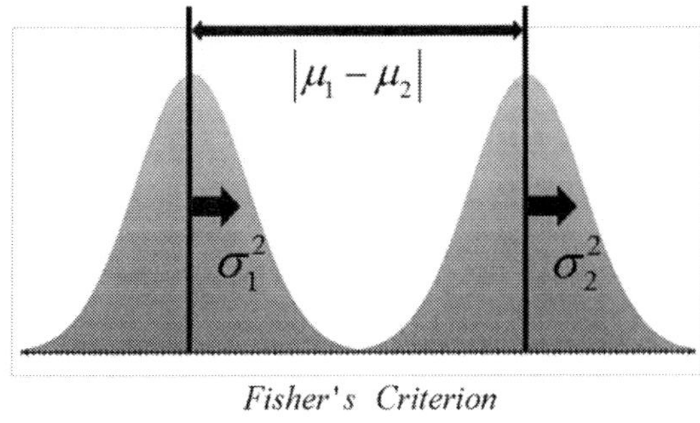

Figure 3. FC Ratio Schematic Diagram

Lastly, the K-means algorithm will be used to set up the threshold for identifying the key parameters. As a clustering method, K-means proposed by MacQueen [4] is a type of unsupervised learning algorithms, which solves the problem of clustering unlabeled data. The goal of this algorithm is to partition the data into ***K*** groups, and assign a cluster to each data point; ***K*** represents the number of clusters.

The procedure of the K-means algorithm and its flow chart (see Figure 4) are shown as follows:

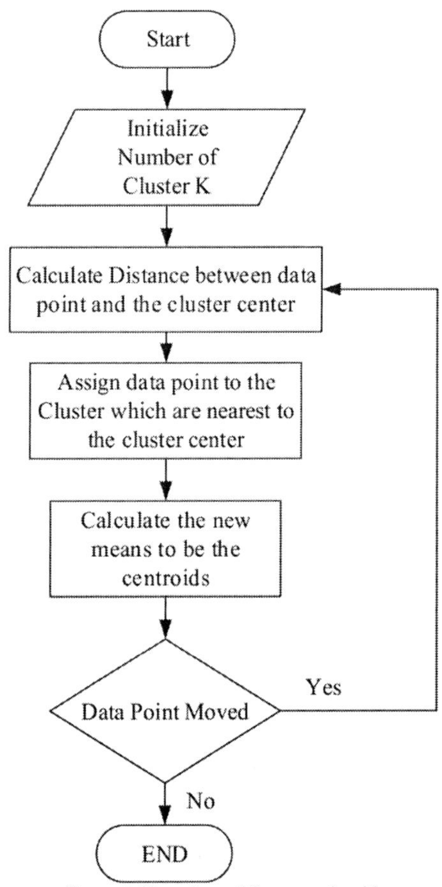

Figure 4. Flow chart of K-means algorithm

1. Select K the number of clusters;
2. Assign each data point to the clusters that has the nearest to the cluster center;
3. Updated the new means of each cluster;
4. Repeat Steps 2 and 3 until no data point moved.

In addition, Figure 5 illustrates the proposed key parameter identification process.

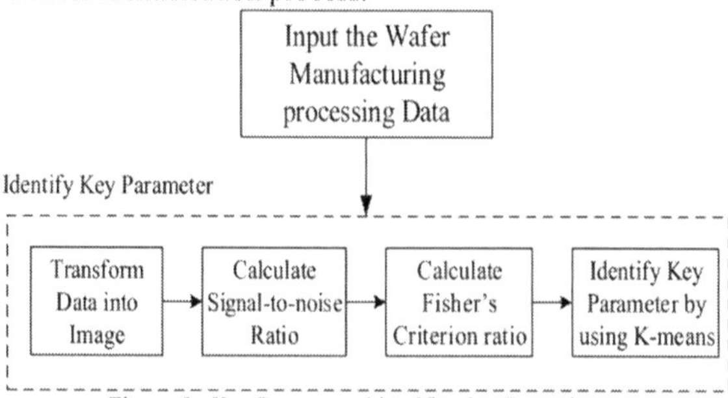

Figure 5. Key Parameter Identification Procedure.

In the next section, some preliminary experimental results are demonstrated to validate the proposed procedure.

II. Experimental Results of Key Parameter Idendification

The key parameter identification result will be presented in this section. Every parameter was investigated by using the proposed procedure. An exemplary parameter, Chamber heater pid error, is illustrated in Figure 6. In the table, the original data profile is shown in (a), and the image representation in (b). In (a), the red lines indicate the profiles of the defective wafers, whereas the blue lines represent the profiles of the good wafers.

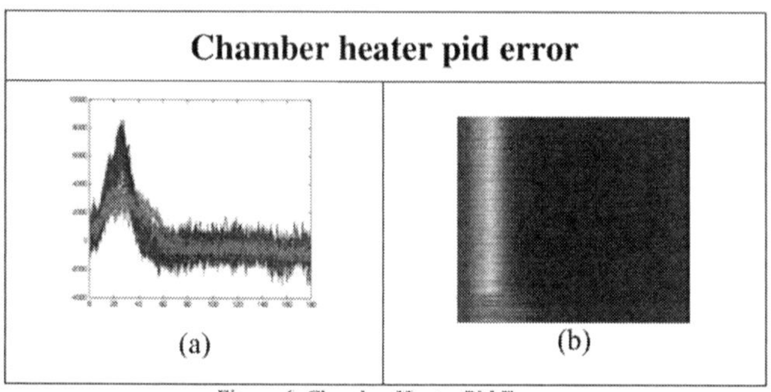

Figure 6. Chamber Heater Pid Error.

In this study, potential key parameters are mainly identified based upon Fisher's Criterion, and then Table I tabulates the FC values of all the 38 parameters. To set up a threshold for identification, the K-mean algorithm is used to classify all the 38 FC values into two clusters: key parameters and non-key parameters. As mentioned in subsection *D*, the cluster with a larger FC value is deemed the key parameter cluster.

TABLE I. FISHER'S CRITERION LISTS OF 38 PARAMETERS

Parameter	Fisher's Criterion
1. BufPurge N2 MFC Flow	0.03922
2. Buffer Chamber Robot Correct EXT	0.10435
3. Buffer Chamber Robot Correct ROT	0.01229
4. CHILLED WATER TEMP	0.01998
5. CH Inner Heater Zone Temp	3.74436
6. CH Outer Heater Voltage Ratio Mode	0.001468
7. Chamber heater pid error	5.01448
8. H2_Flow Setpoint1	0.001038
9. H2_MFCFlow	0.000226
10. Heater servo fwd	0
11. N2 Flow Setpoint1	0.009865
12. N2 MFC Flow	0.009985
13. N2 PURGE Flow Setpoint1	0.022763
14. N2 PURGE_MFC Flow	0.01684
15. NF3_MFCFlow	0.013256
16. Number Wafer In Periodic Clean Process	0
⋮	⋮

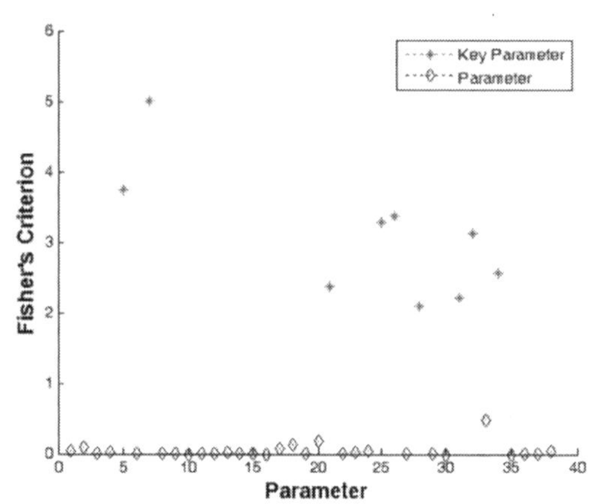

Figure 7. Identify Key Parameter by Using K-means.

Figure 7 exhibits the classification result via K-means as $K=2$. The red points denote the key parameters as the black point represents the non-key parameters. In the figure, the Y axis stands for the FC value and the X axis denotes the parameter ID. The identified 9 key parameters are also shown in Table II. The identified parameters are all related to the inner heater sensors, which were also confirmed by the on-site engineers. Based upon this process investigation, the process engineer can proceed to constructing adequate control charts for a much smaller set of process parameters. By doing so, the false alarm of FDC can be greatly reduced.

TABLE II. KEY PARAMETERS IDENTIFIED

Result of Research Method	Engineer's Experience
Chamber heater pid error	✓
Chamber Inner Heater Zone Current	✓
Chamber Inner Heater Zone Power	✓
Chamber Inner Heater Zone Voltage	✓
⋮	⋮

III. CONCLUSION

In this research, the proposed method clearly identifies 9 key parameters. This result concurs by the well-known process engineer's domain knowledge and practical experiences. Through this case study, the proposed method proves to be a viable tool capable of correctly identifying the key parameters out of abundant process parameters in the semiconductor manufacturing practice. An immediate study for future research could be the identification of possible key steps for the key parameters revealed from this paper.

REFERENCES

[1] M. S. Bartlett, J. R. Movellan, and T. J. Sejnowski, "Face Recognition by independent component analysis," IEEE Transactions on Neural Networks, Vol. 13, No. 6, pp. 1450-1464, 2002.

[2] R. O. Duda, P. E. Hart and D. G. Stork, "Pattern classification," Wiley, New York, 2001.

[3] G. Pires, U. Nuness and M. Castelo-Branco,"Statistical spatialfiltering for a P300-based BCI: Tests in able-bodied, and patients with cerebral palsy and amyotrophic lateral sclerosis," Journal of Neuroscience Methods, Vol. 195, pp. 270-281, 2011.

[4] J. MacQueen, "Some methods for classification and analysis of multivariate observations" In Proceedings of the fifth Berkeley symposium on mathematical statistics and probability, Vol. 1, No. 14, pp. 281-297, 1967.

[5] D. R. Mackay, "The impact of EDI on the components sector of the Australian automotive industry," The Journal of Strategic Information Systems, Vol. 2, No. 3, pp. 243-263, 1993.

Minimizing LR(1) State Machines is NP-Hard

Wuu Yang

Computer Science Department
National Chiao-Tung University
Taiwan, R.O.C.

***Abstract*—LR(1) parsing was a focus of extensive research years ago. Though most fundamental mysteries have been resolved, a few remain hidden in the dark corners. The one we bumped into is the minimization of the LR(1) state machines, which we prove is NP-hard. It is the node-coloring problem that is reduced to the minimization puzzle. The reduction makes use of a technique in constructing a context-free grammar from the graph to be colored. The expected LR(1) state machine is derived from the constructed context-free grammar. A minimized LR(1) machine can be used to recover a minimum coloring of the original graph.**

Keywords—graph coloring; LR(1) parser; LALR(1) parser; minimize LR(1) state machine; node coloring; NP-hardness; parsing.

I. Introduction

Parsing is a basic step in every compiler and interpreter. LR parsers are powerful enough to handle almost all practical programming languages [11]. The downside of LR parsers is the huge table size. This caused the development of several variants, such as LALR parsers, which require significantly smaller tables at the expense of reduced capability.

The core of an LR(1) parser is a deterministic finite state machine. The LALR(1) state machine may be obtained by merging *every* pair of similar states(Note that two states are *similar* if and only if they become identical if the look-ahead sets in the items in the two states are ignored.) in the LR(1) machine [8]. In case (reduce-reduce) conflicts occur due to merging,(note that only reduce-reduce conflicts may occur due to merging similar states.) the parser is forced to revert to the larger, original LR(1) machine. Due to the significant size difference between LR(1) and LALR(1) state machines, we know there are many pairs of similar states in an LR(1) machine. If any pair of similar states may cause conflicts, the parser will be forced to use the much larger LR(1) machine. It would be more reasonable to merge some, but not all, pairs of similar states [16]. The result, called an *extended LALR(1) state machine*, is smaller than the LR(1) machine but larger than the LALR(1) machine.

For example, there are five pairs of similar states in the LR(1) machine in Figure 1. Only three pairs—$(s_1, t_1), (s_2, t_2), (s_3, t_3)$—can be merged. The pair of similar states—(s_5, t_5)—cannot be merged due to a (reduce-reduce) conflict. The last pair of similar states—(s_4, t_4)—cannot be merged because (s_5, t_5) are not merged for otherwise the resulting machine would become nondeterministic. Figure 2 is the corresponding (minimum) LR(1) machine.

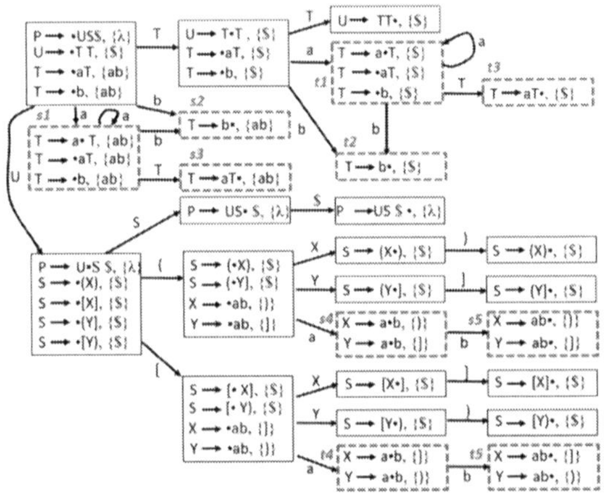

Fig. 1. The LR(1) machine of a grammar.

In general, two states in an LR(1) machine can be merged if and only if the following two conditions are satisfied:

1) The two states must be similar;
2) Corresponding successor states of the two states must have already been merged.

A further question is if there is an efficient algorithm that can merge the *most* number of similar states, thus producing a *minimum* LR(1) state machine. That is, we wish to minimize the LR(1) state machine. Since the number of similar states is finite, a naïve approach is to try all possibilities.

Our study shows that minimizing the LR(1) state machine is an NP-hard problem. We reduce the node-coloring problem to this minimization problem. Starting from an (undirected) graph to be node-colored, we construct a context-free grammar. Then the LR(1) machine of the context-free grammar is derived. We can use an algorithm to calculate the corresponding minimum LR(1) machine.

In order to recover a minimum coloring from this minimum LR(1) machine, we can perform one more easy step. In the LR(1) machine, every state that is not similar to any other states is removed, leaving only similar states. Then an edge between two similar states is added if the two similar states may cause conflicts. The resulting machine is called a *conflict graph*. Merging similar states in the LR(1) machine is essentially identical to merging states in the conflict graph. (Note that Due to the construction of the grammar, all states

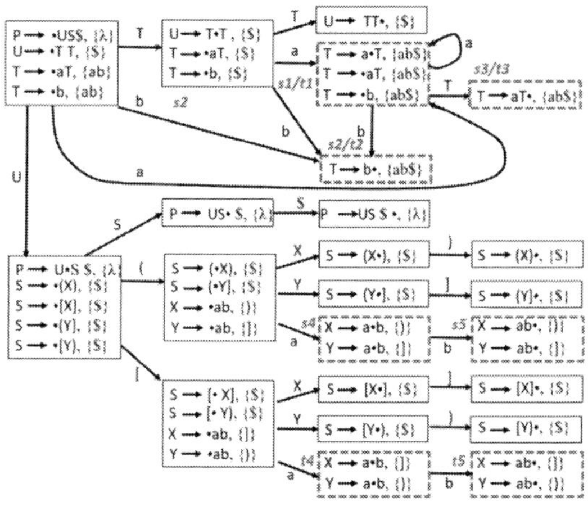

Fig. 2. The corresponding minimum LR(1) machine for Figure 1.

in the resulting conflict graph are similar to one another in the LR(1) machine. Furthermore, the conflict graph is actually isomorphic to the original color graph.) From the minimum LR(1) machine, it is straightforward to recover a minimum coloring.

The following theorem seems obvious but we wish to bring it to the reader's attention when reading this paper:

Theorem. *Let s_1, s_2, and s_3 be three similar states in an LR(1) machine. If the three states are not conflicting pairwise, then merging all three states will not create any conflicts.*

Due to the above theorem, we need to consider only pairs, not triples, quadruples, *etc.*, of similar states. This greatly simplifies our discussion.

Note also that there might be more than one minimum LR(1) machine for a given LR(1) machine.

LR parsers were first introduced by Knuth [11]. Since LR parsers are considered the most powerful and efficient practical parsers, much effort has been devoted to related research and implementation [1][3][7][10][12][14].

It is known that every language that admits an LR(k) parser also admits an LALR(1) parser [12]. In order to parse for an LR(1)-but-non-LALR(1) grammar, there used to be four approaches: (1) use the much larger LR(1) parser; (2) add ad hoc rules to the LALR(1) parser to resolve conflicts, similar to what yacc [10] does; (3) merge some, but not all, pairs of similar states [16]; and (4) transform the grammar into LALR(1) and then generate a parser. The transformation approach may exponentially increase the number of production rules [12] and the transformed grammar is usually difficult to understand. This paper shows that, although we wish to merge as many pairs of similar states as possible, this optimization problem is NP-hard.

Pager proposed two methods: "practical general method" (PGM) [14] and "lane-tracing method" [13] [15]. Chen [4] actually implements Pager's two methods as well as other improvements, such as unit-production elimination. Because

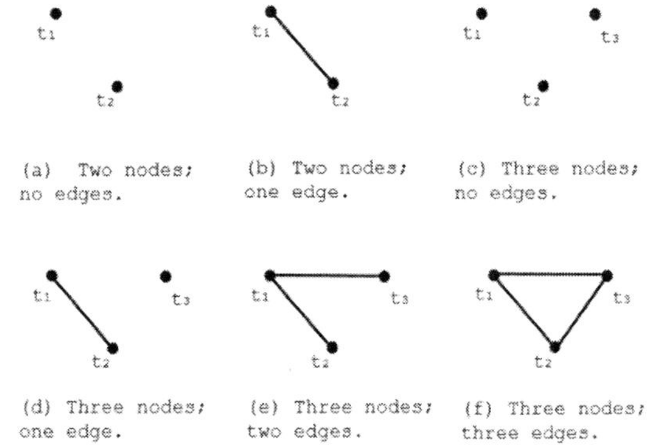

Fig. 3. Two cases for a color graph with two nodes and four cases for a color graph with three nodes.

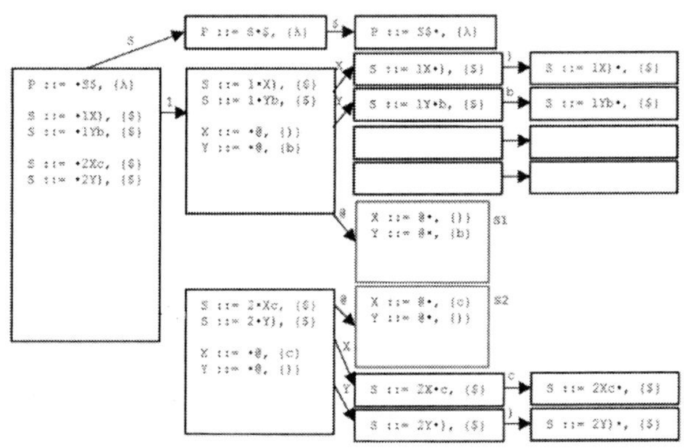

Fig. 4. The LR(1) machine for the graph in Figure 3 (b). Note that there is a single conflict $s_1 \leftrightarrow s_2$. The empty boxes are not part of this machine. They are used for comparison with later machines.

the minimization problem is NP-hard, it is important to build practical LR parser generators. Pager and Chen's work is one of the best existing LR parser generators. The IELR method [5] includes additional capability to eliminate conflicts even if the grammar is not LR.

Both [14] and [5] attempt to find a *minimal* machine. However, *minimal* simply means "very small" or "locally minimum" rather than "globally minimum"[5]. This is different from our study of *minimization*.

The remainder of this paper is organized as follows. Section 2 will introduce the terminology and background. Section 3 introduces a reduction algorithm that translates an undirected graph into a context-free grammar and discusses the reduction of the coloring problem to the minimization problem. The last section concludes this paper.

II. Terminology and Background

A grammar $G = (N, T, P, S)$ consists of a non-empty set of nonterminals N, a non-empty set of terminals T, a non-empty set of production rules P and a special nonterminal S, which is called the start symbol. We assume that $N \cap T = \emptyset$.

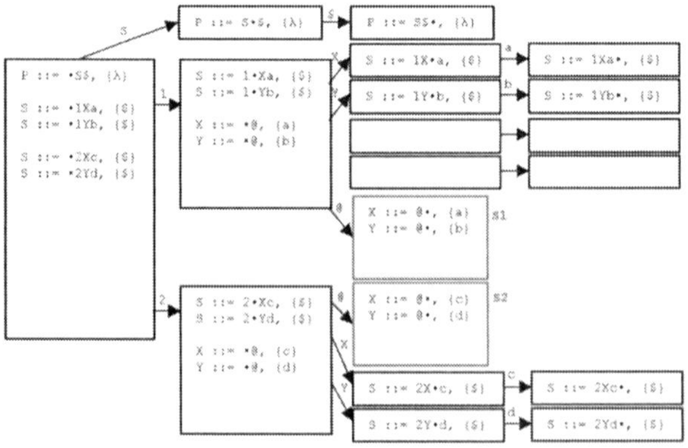

Fig. 5. The LR(1) machine for the graph in Figure 3 (a). There is no conflict in the machine. The empty boxes are not part of this machine. They are used for comparison with later machines. G32-0.

LR(1) parsing is based on a deterministic finite state machine, called the LR(1) machine. A state in the LR(1) machine is a non-empty set of items. An *item* has the form (A ::= γ_1 • γ_2, la), where A ::= $\gamma_1\gamma_2$ is one of the production rules, • indicates a position in the string $\gamma_1\gamma_2$, and la (the *lookahead* set) is a set of terminals that could follow the nonterminal A in later derivation steps. The algorithm for constructing the LR(1) state machine for a grammar is explained in most compiler textbooks, for example, [2][8]. An example state machine is shown in Figure 1.

Two states in the LR(1) machine are *similar* if they have the same number of items and the corresponding items differ only in the lookahead sets. For example, states $s1$ and $t1$ in Figure 1, each of which contains three items, are similar states.

LR(1) state machines are closely related to LR(0) state machines. However, an LR(1) machine is much larger than the corresponding LR(0) machine because many similar states are introduced. In order to reduce the size of the LR(1) state machine, some or all pairs of similar states may be *merged* as long as no conflicts occur. For example, LALR(1) machines are obtained from LR(1) machines by merging *every* pair of similar states.

Sometimes merging two similar states may create a *(parsing) conflict*. The aim of *minimizing an LR(1) machine* is to merge as many pairs of similar states as possible without causing conflicts. Our study shows that this minimization problem is NP-hard.

III. Reduction

We may prove that minimizing LR(1) machines is an NP-hard problem by reducing the node-coloring problem to this minimization problem. Specifically, from a graph F to be colored, we construct a context-free grammar G. Then the LR(1) state machine M is derived from G. An algorithm is used to calculate the minimum state machine, from which a minimum coloring can be recovered.

(no edge)	(one edge)
P ::= S$	P ::= S$
S ::= 1Xa	S ::= 1X)
S ::= 1Yb	S ::= 1Yb
S ::= 2Xc	S ::= 2Xc
S ::= 2Yd	S ::= 2Y)
X ::= @	X ::= @
Y ::= @	Y ::= @

Fig. 6. The two grammars the color graphs in Figure 3 (a) and (b).

(a)	(b)	(c)	(d)
P ::= S$	P ::= S$	P ::= S$	P ::= S$
S ::= 1Xa	S ::= 1X)	S ::= 1X)	S ::= 1X)
S ::= 1Yb	S ::= 1Yb	S ::= 1Yb	S ::= 1Yb
S ::= 1Ze	S ::= 1Ze	S ::= 1Z=	S ::= 1Z=
S ::= 1Vf	S ::= 1Vf	S ::= 1Vf	S ::= 1Vf
S ::= 2Xc	S ::= 2Xc	S ::= 2Xc	S ::= 2Xc
S ::= 2Yd	S ::= 2Y)	S ::= 2Y)	S ::= 2Y)
S ::= 2Zg	S ::= 2Zg	S ::= 2Zg	S ::= 2Z=
S ::= 2Vh	S ::= 2Vh	S ::= 2Vh	S ::= 2Vh
S ::= 3Xi	S ::= 3Xi	S ::= 3Xi	S ::= 3Xi
S ::= 3Yj	S ::= 3Yj	S ::= 3Yj	S ::= 3Yj
S ::= 3Zk	S ::= 3Zk	S ::= 3Zk	S ::= 3Zk
S ::= 3Vm	S ::= 3Vm	S ::= 3V=	S ::= 3V=
X ::= @	X ::= @	X ::= @	X ::= @
Y ::= @	Y ::= @	Y ::= @	Y ::= @
Z ::= @	Z ::= @	Z ::= @	Z ::= @
V ::= @	V ::= @	V ::= @	V ::= @

Fig. 7. The four grammars constructed from graphs with 3 nodes by our algorithm.

In order to recover a minimum coloring, M can be simplified by removing every state that is not similar to any other state, resulting in a *conflict graph*. Merging similar states in the conflict graph is essentially identical to finding a minimum coloring of F.

We define a *node-coloring of a graph* as a partition of the set of nodes in the color graph satisfying the requirement that nodes connected by an edge cannot be in the same partition block. A *minimum coloring* is a partition with the fewest blocks. Similarly, a *merge scheme* of an LR(1) state machine is a partition of the states satisfying the requirement that states in the same partition block are similar to one another and do not conflict with one another. A *minimum merge scheme* is a partition with the fewest blocks. *Minimizing an LR(1) machine* is to find a minimum merge scheme of the machine.

We build a context-free grammar G for a given color graph F *inductively*.

Assume color graph F has n nodes. Then the constructed machine M has n states that are similar to one another; the remaining states are distinct and can be ignored in the discussion of merging similar states. There is 1-1 correspondence between the n nodes in F and the n similar states in M. We claim that M satisfies the following property:

> *F may be colored with k colors if and only if $n-k$ pairs of similar states in M may be merged (so that only k similar states remain).*

If there is any algorithm that can calculate the minimum LR(1) machine M_{min} from M by merging certain pairs of similar states, we can use that algorithm to solve the node-coloring problem—for all states that are merged into a single state in M_{min}, their corresponding nodes in F have the same color.

Due to the above property, we have successfully reduced the node-coloring problem to the minimization problem. Because the node-coloring problem is NP-hard [9], the minimization problem is also NP-hard.

To construct a context-free grammar from the color graph F, we first choose two arbitrary nodes t_1 and t_2. There are two cases, shown in Figure 3 (a) and (b): there is no or one edge t_1—t_2. Then one of the grammars in Figure 6 is selected.

Assume that there is an edge t_1—t_2 in F. Then the grammar on the right inFigure 6 is selected. The corresponding LR(1) machine is shown in Figure 4, in which there are two similar states (s_1 and s_2). Merging the two similar states will cause a conflict due to the terminal symbol ")". The grammar is carefully constructed so that the conflict $s_1 \leftrightarrow s_2$ corresponds to the edge t_1—t_2 in F.

In our constructed grammars, the numbers, such as 1, 2, 14, 27, *etc.*, are teminals and indicate a similar state in the resulting LR(1) machine and the order the corresponding nodes in F are chosen. The upper-case English letters, such as A, B, *etc.*, denote nonterminals. The lower-case English letters, such as a, b, *etc.*, denote terminals that are used only once in the grammar. These lower-case letters will not cause conflicts. The punctuation marks, such as ")" and "=", are terminals that will cause conflicts.

On the other hand, if t_1 and t_2 in F are not connected, the grammar on the left in Figure 6 will be selected. Figure 5 is the LR(1) machine for that grammar. There are two similar states in that machine (s_1 and s_2). The two similar states can be merged without conflicts. This corresponds to the fact that t_1 and t_2 in Figure 3 (a) can have the same color since there is no edge connecting them.

Note that the notion of *"two (similar) states can be merged"* in the LR(1) machine is closely related to the notion of *"two nodes can have there same color"* due to our construction.

The remaining nodes in F are chosen one by one in an arbitrary order. By adding one node at a time, we can gradually construct grammars $G_2, G_3, G_4, \ldots, G_n$. The complete algorithm for generating a context-free grammar from a graph is shown in Figure 10.

Example. The grammar on the right column in Figure 6 is extended to the grammar on the third column in Figure 7. The four grammars constructed from graphs with 3 nodes by our algorithm. (a) is for graphs with no edges (Figure 3 (c)); (b) is for graphs with one edge (Figure 3 (d)); (c) is for graphs with two edges (Figure 3 (e)); and (d) is for graphs with three edges (Figure 3 (f)). The production rules are classified into five categories. In particular, the boxed production rules in (c) are new rules added to the grammar on the right column in Figure 6.The corresponding color graphs are shown in Figure 3 (b) and (e), respectively. The boxed production rules are added by the algorithm in Figure 10. □

The grammar on the third column in Figure 7 is a typical grammar generated by our algorithm. The production rules are classified into five categories:

1) one starting production rule (*i.e.*, P ::= S $)
2) four production rules of the form (Π ::= @)
3) four production rules whose right-hand sides begin with the terminal 1
4) four production rules whose right-hand sides begin with the terminal 2
5) four production rules whose right-hand sides begin with the terminal 3

The LR(1) machine is then derived from the grammar. We did not construct the LR(1) machines directly because context-free grammars are easier to generate.

Now consider the constructed LR(1) machine in Figure 9. Note that all items derived from rules of categories 1, 3, 4, and 5, appear only once in the whole LR(1) machine. Any state containing any of these items will not be similar to any other state and hence can be ignored. We could focus on states consisting solely of items derived from production rules of category 2. There are only 3 such states, which are indeed similar to one another. Each such state has all items of the form (Π ::= @ •, ...), where Π is a nonterminal except P and S.

Another characteristic of the constructed LR(1) machine in Figure 9 is that there are no cycles. The longest path contains 3 steps.

In fact, all grammars generated by the algorithm in Figure 10 share the above characteristics. They help us to infer properties of the minimized LR(1) machines.

In the corresponding state machine in Figure 9, consider the four states that come immediately after the initial state. Items derived from rules in categories (3), (4) and (5) are cleanly separated because of the first symbols (which are integer terminals) on the right-hand sides of the rules. Hence, except the four states that come immediately after the initial state, those items whose first symbols on the right-hand sides are different will never be mixed in the same state in the state machine. Items derived from rules in category (2) are quite similar—actually all items of the form (Π ::= • @, where is Π is a nonterminal) appear in every state that comes immediately after the initial state (we will ignore the starting production

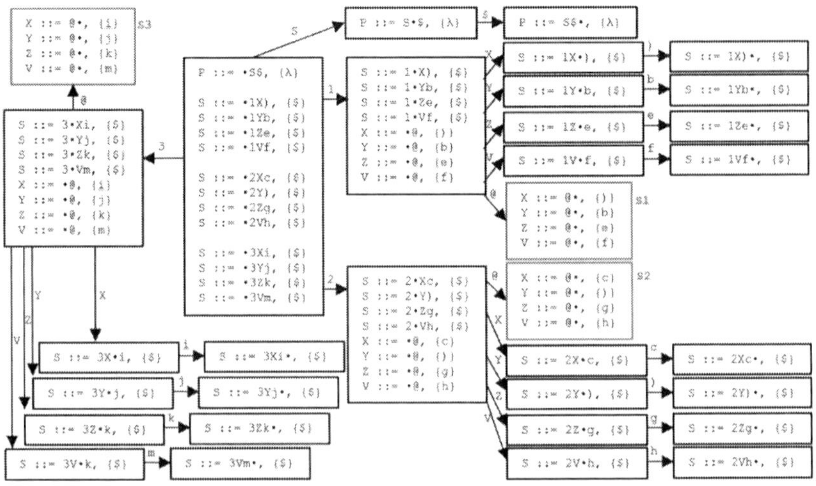

Fig. 8. The LR(1) machine for the graph in Figure 3 (d).

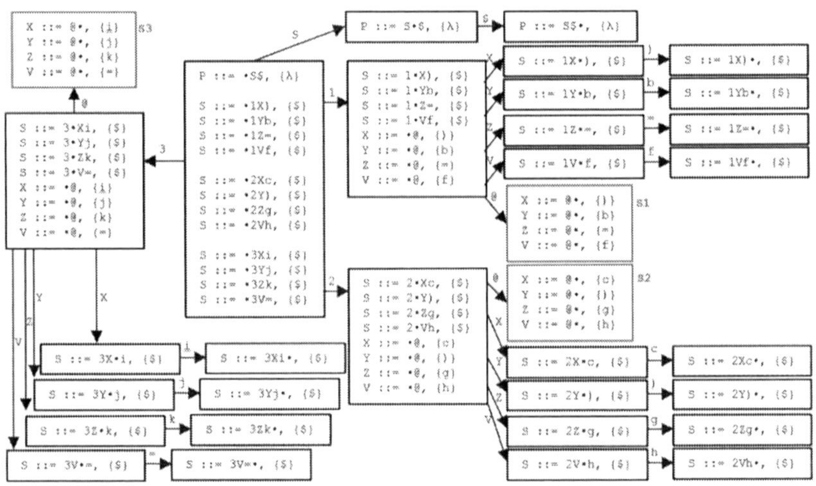

Fig. 9. The LR(1) machine for the graph in Figure 3 (e).

rule in this discussion). Furthermore, all items of the form (Π ::= @ •) appear in states that come two steps after the initial state. It is these states (which contain all items of the form (Π ::= @ •) and no other items) that are similar to one another. All other states are not similar to any other states and hence can be ignored when we discuss the merging of similar states.

Therefore, we can create or avoid conflicts among similar states by carefully adjusting the last terminal ψ in rules of the form (S ::= μ Π ψ), where μ is an integer terminal, Π is a nonterminal, and ψ is a terminal. In the four grammars in Figure 7, when ψ is a lower-case English letter (*e.g.*, "b" or "i"), that rule will not cause any conflict because the lower-case letter appears only once in the whole grammar. On the other hand, when ψ is a punctuation marks (*e.g.*, ")" or "="), a conflict is intentionally added to the grammar because that punctuation mark is used in two different production rules. The above discussion is related lines 18-22 in the algorithm in Figure 10.

We will use an algorithm to calculate the minimum state machine from M.

In what follows, we will describe how to recover a minimum coloring of the original color graph from the minimum state machine.

For the purpose of merging similar states, we may ignore all states that are not similar to any other states. To make conflicts among states explicit we add a *conflict edge* between two states if a conflict will occur when the two states are merged. The state machine in Figure 9 becomes Figure 11, which is called a *conflict graph*. In Figure 11, there are two conflict edges $s_1 \leftrightarrow s_2$ and $s_1 \leftrightarrow s_3$.

Finding a minimum merge scheme for the LR(1) machine is identical to finding a minimum merge scheme for the conflict graph. So we will focus on the conflict graph instead.

```
1.  Nodes in graph P are listed as v1, v2, ..., vn;
2.  if there is an edge v1—v2 then G := the left grammar in Figure 6 ;
3.  else G := the right grammar in Figure 6;
4.  NewNonTerm := { X, Y };
5.  for μ := 3 to n do
6.      generate two new nonterminals, called Δ and Θ;
7.      generate two new terminals, called φ and ω;
8.      generate four production rules:
9.          ("S ::= " μ Δ φ) and ("S ::= " μ Θ ω) and
10.         (Δ " ::= @") and (Θ " ::= @");
11.     for each nonterminal Π ∈ NewNonTerm do
12.         generate a new terminal, called ψ;
13.         generate a production rule: ("S ::= " μ Π ψ);
14.     end;
15.     for δ := 1 to μ − 1 do
16.         generate two new terminals, called τ and ρ;
17.         generate a production rule: ("S ::= " δ Θ ρ);
18.         if there is an edge vμ ↔ vδ then
19.             /* The following rule will cause a conflict due to ω. */
20.             generate a production rule: ("S ::= " δ Δ ω);
21.         else /* The following rule will NOT cause a conflict. */
22.             generate a production rule: ("S ::= " δ Δ τ);
23.     end;
24.     NewNonTerm := NewNonTerm ∪ {Δ, Θ};
25. end;
```

Fig. 10. Algorithm for generating a context-free grammar from a graph. The four rules generated at lines 9, 17, and 20 will cause a conflict in the LR(1) machine due to the terminal ω.

Fig. 11. The conflict graph. After removing the states that are not similar to any other states, only three states are left. We may add an edge $s_1 \leftrightarrow s_2$ to indicate there is a conflict edge $s_1 \leftrightarrow s_2$ and another conflict edge $s_1 \leftrightarrow s_3$.

The reader may find that the conflict graph (Figure 11) is isomorphic to the original color graph (Figure 3 (e)). This is due to the construction of the context-free grammar.

IV. Conclusion

We have reduced the node-coloring problem to the minimization problem of the LR(1) state machines. Therefore, the minimization problem is NP-hard.

There are efficient algorithms for minimization of finite state machines. LR(0) state machines are minimum by its construction. We show that LR(1) state machines cannot be easily minimized in general.

Note that minimizing an LR(1) machine is quite different from minimizing a general finite state machine. For one thing, we need to examine the items in the states of an LR(1) machine. On the other hand, minimizing a general finite state machine does not consider the "contents" of the states.

Acknowledgement

This work is supported, in part, by Ministry of Science and Technology, Taiwan, R.O.C., under contracts MOST 103-2221-E-009-105-MY3 and MOST 105-2221-E-009-078-MY3.

References

[1] A.V. Aho and S.C. Johnson. "LR Parsing," ACM Computing Surveys, vol. 6, no. 2, June 1974. pp. 99-124.
[2] A.V. Aho, M.S. Lam, R. Sethi, and J.D. Ullman. Compilers: Principles, Techniques, and Tools. (2nd Edition) Prentice Hall, New York, 2006.
[3] T. Anderson, J. Eve, and J. Horning. "Efficient LR(1) parsers," Acta Informatica, vol. 2, 1973. pp. 2-39.
[4] X. Chen and D. Pager. "Full LR(1) Parser Generator Hyacc And Study On The Performance of LR(1) Algorithms." In Proc. 4th International C* Conf. Computer Science and Software Engineering (C3S2E '11), May 16-18, Montreal, CANADA, 2011. pp. 83-92.
[5] J.E. Denny and B.A. Malloy. "IELR(1) algorithm for generating minimal LR(1) parser tables for non-LR(1) grammars with conflict resolution," Science of Computer Programming, vol. 75, no. 11, November 2010. pp. 943-979. doi:10.1016/j.scico.2009.08.001.
[6] F.L. DeRemer. Practical translators for LR(k) languages. Project MAC Tech. Rep. TR-65, MIT, Cambridge, Mass., 1969.
[7] F.L. DeRemer. "Simple LR(k) Grammars." Comm. ACM, vol. 14, no. 7, July 1971. pp. 453-460.
[8] C.N. Fischer, R.K. Cytron, and R.J. LeBlanc, Jr.. Crafting A Compiler. Pearson, New York, 2010.
[9] M.R. Garey and D.S. Johnson. Computers and Intractability: A Guide to the Theory of NP-Completeness. W. H. Freeman, 1979. ISBN 0-7167-1045-5.
[10] S.C. Johnson. Yacc: Yet Another Compiler-Compiler. Bell Laboratories, Murray Hill, NJ, 1978.
[11] D. E. Knuth. "On the translation of languages from left to right." Information and Control, vol. 8, no. 6, July 1965. pp. 607-639. doi:10.1016/S0019-9958(65)90426-2.
[12] M.D. Mickunas, R.L. Lancaster, V.B. Schneider. "Transforming LR(k) Grammars to LR(1), SLR(1), and (1,1) Bounded Right-Context Grammars." Journal of the ACM, vol. 23, no. 3, July 1976. pp. 511-533. doi:10.1145/321958.321972.
[13] D. Pager. "The lane tracing algorithm for constructing LR(k) parsers." In Proc 5th Annual ACM Symp. Theory of computing, Austin, Texas, United States, 1973. pp. 172181.
[14] D. Pager. "A practical general method for constructing LR(k) parsers." Acta Informatica, vol. 7, no. 3, 1977. pp. 249-268. doi:10.1007/BF00290336.
[15] D. Pager. "The lane-tracing algorithm for constructing LR(k) parsers and ways of enhancing its efficiency." Information Sciences, vol. 12, 1977. pp. 1942.
[16] W. Yang, "Extended LALR(1) Parsing." In Proc. 13th International Conf. Autonomic and Autonomous Systems (ICAS 2017), May 21-25, 2017. Barcelona, Spain.

Unmanned Aerial System Operations for Retail

Guido Manfredi, Elgiz Baskaya, Jim Sharples and Yannick Jestin
ENGIE Ineo - Groupe ADP - SAFRAN RPAS Chair
Universite de Toulouse, Ecole Nationale d'Aviation Civile
Toulouse, France
Email: guido.manfredi@enac.fr

***Abstract*—The number of Unmanned Aerial System (UAS) applications is quickly increasing as technology, standards and regulation allow them. With each new application, more industrial sectors get affected, and the retail sector is already being impacted. This paper presents five UAS applications that will impact the retail sector: freight, monitoring, guiding, delivery, and advertisement. For each application, concepts of operation are provided along with the associated technological, standard and regulatory locks. These operations are then organized along time, from earliest to latest accessible, with accompanying explanation as to why and when. It is shown that the applications currently most publicized are not the ones that will come first. Finally, a discussion regarding the accuracy of our forecast is proposed and leads to support the enabling of drones, in the retail sector, are provided.**

***Keywords*–UAS; RPAS; drones; retail; mass distribution; integration; drone operations.**

I. Introduction

The retail sector has been quickly evolving in the last decades, as it aptly integrated emerging technologies. The advent of the Internet enabled big data and machine learning approaches, e.g., recommender systems based on customers browsing history to target advertisement [1]; automation changed the way general merchandise stores worked with self-checkout machines and automated drive supermarkets [2]. Smart sensors changed the way online retail stores present their goods, with the development of virtual dressing rooms [3]. Even the most complex technologies have been integrated in the retail sector, with warehouse robots allowing fast and efficient content management [4] and robotic guides improving the customers' experience [5]. The successive technologies transformed the industry in many ways by changing how goods are stored and managed, reducing the number of intermediates, automating dull and dirty tasks, and changing the customers' habits and experience. Now, a new technology is about to become fully available: Unmanned Aerial Systems (UAS). A well-known example is the Amazon prototype [6] for autonomous package delivery. However, there are lesser known applications, which could have more impact on the retail industry and sooner than one might think.

This paper studies five applications in which UAS operations will impact the retail sector. For each application, different concepts of operation are considered. For each operation type, the key enablers are listed. Exemples of such operations, and ongoing research on the topic, are also provided. As the reader may not be familiar with UASs, Section II introduces their architectures, their environment, and their regulation. With this information in mind, Section III presents the five applications along with the technologies and regulation required to enable them. Tentative dates at which these applications will become possible are provided in Section IV. Finally, the conclusion provides future leads to explore in order to enable UAS operations for retail.

II. The UAS World

There are numerous words to designate drones, each with its own meaningful nuance. For the sake of clarity, in the rest of this paper, we use indifferently the terms UAS and drones, with the definitions provided hereafter.

A. *UAS Architecture*

The S in UAS stands for "System", a UAS is composed of three elements: an Unmanned Aerial Vehicle (UAV), a Command and Control link (C2 link), and a Ground Control Station (GCS). We provide some general information regarding each one of these elements, as it will be useful to understand the limitations in different applications.

1) UAV: The UAV is the aerial part of the UAS. There are numerous ways to categorize UAVs. For clarity we will consider that they can belong to one of three families: rotorcraft, fixed wind, and airship. The most represented type of UAV is the rotorcraft. It does not have wings and entirely relies on the thrust from its propellers to fly. Easy to pilot, especially for take-off and landing, it allows the pilot precise positioning. Its drawback is the energy needed to remain aloft, as well as the noise and wind created by the propulsion. With low endurance, it remains the most popular form of UAV. The fixed wing UAV flies thanks to the lift produced by the flow of air above its wings, like most manned airplanes. For this reason, it must remain inside a given flight envelope and is thus less maneuverable than rotorcrafts. As the lift comes from the air reaction and not purely from the propellers' thrust, it has high endurance and can fly for long periods of time. Plus, it can carry high payload relative to its own weight. It needs an initial speed for takeoff, and some distance for landing, though it is possible to design Vertical Take Off and Landing (VTOL) fixed wing aircraft, greatly simplifying the beginning and end of flight. Its aerodynamic shape allows it to reach high speeds. For a airship type UAV, the majority of its lift comes from a lighter-than-air gas inside its structure allowing it to stay aloft with energy spent only for motion. Consequently, it has the highest endurance of the three types. However, having to store gas onboard gives it a bulky shape which reduces the maximum speed/maneuverability and makes it sensitive to external perturbations (e.g., wind). The UAV also carries the equipage, i.e., the onboard equipment needed for the UAS operation (e.g., flight, rules compliance) but not necessary to perform its assigned task. The equipage comprises the sensors

TABLE I. PERFORMANCES OF DIFFERENT UAV TYPES.

UAV type	Rotorcraft	Fixed-wing	Airship
Endurance	Low	High	Very high
Speed	Medium	High	Low
Manoeuvrability	Very high	Medium	Low
Payload	Medium	High	Low
Cost	Medium	Very low	Low

used to navigate (e.g., GPS, cameras), the communication systems, and the equipment required by regulation (e.g., lights, sound). A brief summary of the differences between these types of aircraft is provided in Table I.

2) C2 link: The C2 link is the medium used to uplink/downlink Command and Control (C2) data to/from the UAV. From an operation point of view, C2 links can belong to one of three categories: direct link, terrestrial network, satellite network. The direct link allows short range (few kilometers) control over a UAV. It has the benefit of not relying on a service provider. For long range operations, the C2 link can be carried over a terrestrial network. Due to the cost of such installations, a service provider is required. The delay in such type of communication is low enough to be comparable to direct link. Similarly, satellite networks allow very long range operations and operations where no ground network is available (e.g., over mountains, water). But it has longer delay than direct or terrestrial networks. This type of C2 link may not be useable for certain types of operations, e.g., indoor operations. Again, due to the cost of such structures, it requires a service provider.

3) Ground Control Station: The GCS can be a simple remote control, a cockpit sized control room, or even bigger. Its size and complexity is related to the type of UAV and the type of operation. However, as the GCS is not considered a limiting factor, we will not take into account the different types of GCS in the rest of this paper.

The capabilities of a UAS change greatly depending on its type and equipage. These need to be adapted to the type of operation to ensure a safe flight while allowing the UAS to perform its mission. Note that, for a same UAS, the regulatory constraints vary depending on the environment and type of operation.

B. UAS Environment

The environment of an aircraft can be classified based on three elements: the available services, the systems required on the aircraft and the applicable procedures. Services encompass all external support to the operation, like aeronautical meteorology or conflicts management. System requirements designate onboard equipment needed to interact with services, other aircraft, and to ensure proper following of procedures. Procedures are pre-defined behaviors that an aircraft needs to follow in certain airspaces or situations. When considering manned aviation, these three elements form the Air Traffic Management (ATM) system; these same elements, when specific to drone operation, form the U-Space system.

1) ATM: The ATM has a strong safety record due to its numerous services, high system requirements and numerous procedures. As a consequence, integrating in such an environment is complex. Plus, the fact that manned aviation is currently flying in these environments asks for drones to be integrated seamlessly, i.e., a drone should be able to behave like a manned aircraft in every aspect. Drones capable of integrating in the ATM system are likely to be large ones, with performances close to these of existing manned aviation.

2) U-Space: The notion of U-Space encompasses the services and procedures offered to drones to allow their integration. The U-Space is planned to be rolled out in four phases: U1, U2, U3, and U4 [7]. Phase U1will bring e-registration, e-identification, geofencing (don't go in this area) and geocaging (don't leave this area). Phase U2 will set up management of drone operations through flight planning, flight approval, tracking, airspace dynamic information, and procedural interfaces with ATM. In Phase U3, operations in dense areas, capacity management, assistance for conflict detection will be rolled out. Finally Phase U4 will provide integrated services with manned aviation, high levels of automation for all services. When reaching U4, all types of operations, even the most complex ones, will be supported by the U-Space services and procedures. U-Space will provide traffic management for small UAS but also drone specific services for large UAS.

Depending on the type of operation, the drones will have to integrate with: neither, one, or both of these environments. However, the complexity of integrating a drone not only comes from the environment but also from the risk of the operation, as will be explained in the next section.

C. UAS Regulation

In order to provide an unified answer to the problem of regulating UASs, national regulators and industries gathered to create the Joint Authority for Rulemaking on Unmanned Systems (JARUS). This entity, building on the European Aviation Safety Agency (EASA) rules, proposed to split UAS operations based on risk levels. The risk is mainly defined in terms of probabilities to hit a human on the ground, another airspace user or a critical infrastructure. This led to the definition of three operations categories (A, B and C) described below.

1) Category A: Category A encompasses low risk operations, like most of leisure flights and some professional activities. Operations falling in this category do not require an explicit authorization from civil aviation authorities. But, they are subject to strict operational limitations (e.g., no proximity to people, traffic, infrastructures; no dangerous items; one pilot per UAS; no item dropping). These operational limitations are sufficient to mitigate the low risk. Though some professional activities fit in this category, the main goal is to regulate leisure types of operations.

2) Category B: Category B regroups medium risk operations, such as operation beyond visual line of sight (i.e., no visual contact between pilot and UAV during flight). To facilitate the regulation process, a set of scenarios with specific operational limitations are designed. To operate within a scenario, the UAS needs to comply with a list of requirements. For operations outside the scope of the scenarios, a risk analysis must be carried out to show that the existing risks are properly mitigated. To facilitate this risk analysis process, JARUS developed a framework called the Specific Operations Risk Assessment (SORA). The SORA considers threats, which contribute to the risk, and barriers, which mitigate the risk, to evaluate the actual risk of an operation and decide if the resulting mitigated risk is low enough to allow the operation. The risk analysis needs to be validated by the authorities in order to authorize an operation not included in the standard scenarios.

3) Category C: Operations with risk that cannot be mitigated in Category B are evaluated in Category C. These represent high risk operations, for example large cargo delivery in urban areas. These are likely to be operations with a risk close to current manned aviation's one. As such, the aircraft, avionics, pilot/crew and operator will need to be certified in order to fly these operations. The fact that a certification process is involved increases the complexity of the introduction of UAS in these types of operations. Indeed, before being able to certify a piece of equipment, a standard must be developed for this equipment. Standardization can be understood as the process of defining details and minimum requirements for safe and uniform operation across a diverse range of implementations. However, as of today, not all the parts required to fly a UAS have corresponding standards, e.g., Detect And Avoid (DAA) systems, C2 links, pilot training. So, enabling this category of operation requires extra effort and time for the industry to agree on standards. For Category C, harmonization at the International Civil Aviation Organization (ICAO) is planned to allow international operations.

4) The special case of indoors operations: Indoor operations are not regulated by civil aviation authorities, so the above categories do not apply. In fact, indoor operations fall under the responsibility of the operator and usually no risk analysis or certification is required by the authorities.

With a knowledge of the existing technologies, environments, and regulations, next section introduces UAS operations that will impact the retail sector in the near to long term.

III. UAS Applications for Retail

In the following, we consider five domains where the UASs will impact the retail industry and examine the prerequisites for integration, as well as the obstacles faced on the technological, standardization and regulatory levels.

A. Freight

Freight operations involve the transportation of large quantities of goods, which represents the input of most retail stores. Depending on the way suppliers operate, opportunities for the retail sector can change. Thus, an evolution of the freight can have an impact on the retail sectors. In the following we analyze two freight operations: cargo flights transporting goods on long distances and cargo delivery to urban areas.

1) LUCA: Large Unmanned Cargo Aircraft (LUCA) offer economic opportunities, as demonstrated by Collins [8], especially when it comes to long haul point to point, delivery to/from remote places and high value cargo over distances requiring multiple piloting crews. Removing the cockpit will cut costs related to having a crew onboard and the associated maintenance. Plus, the UAV will be freed of dynamical constraints related to the presence of humans onboard (e.g., limited acceleration, turning angles, braking force). This kind of operation will ask for integration in the ATM system. Aircraft performing these missions will fly along pre-determined routes, will have to access airport environments, and to follow specific ATM procedures. Because it will fly in the middle of the traffic, this type of operation is classified as high risk, Category C, and will ask for certification. From a technical point of view, transforming large manned aircraft into UAVs is possible with existing technology; the UAV having the same capabilities as existing aircraft, it will integrate seamlessly with the ATM environment. But it will require to agree on some standards. Notably for the C2 link, DAA and Automated Take Off and Landing (ATOL) equipment. Indeed, long range operations ask for a terrestrial or satellite communication network, collision avoidance is a requirement to fly with the rest of the traffic, and operating in airport environments remotely requires ATOL and auto-taxi (from gate to runway) capabilities. The rest of the equipment remains the same so no additional standardization effort is required. Once these hurdles are removed, this type of operation will be at hand. Using LUCA could even open new opportunities. Indeed, in the context of the SESAR2020 projects [9], experiments have been carried out to determine drone specific trajectories which could facilitate their landing on airports without disturbing the existing traffic. It has been determined that UAVs can use steeper descent angles and sharper turning angles. Added to the fact that there is no human onboard, so less airport services are required, this could open access to more options in terms of airports and available supply routes.

2) Urban freight: Urban is currently defined in some civil aviation instances as an area with a density of population higher than 1295 people per square kilometer (plus a 0.5NM buffer around it). Nowadays, delivery of goods to urban outlets is mainly done with trucks. This brings problems related to traffic, and increases the cities' complexity. Using air transport can simplify the way deliveries are carried out. It would still require some urban planning for the landing sites and air routes, but could remove the impact and dependency on road traffic. Moreover, little infrastructure would be required for operations contrary to trucks, which require at least roads, facilitating delivery to peculiar places (e.g., islands, old cities). Comparatively to what can be done today with helicopters, using a UAV would allow saving space and weight by removing the cockpit. Plus, today's helicopters operations over urban areas are mostly exceptional. Developing an appropriate regulation for UAS will allow them to operate routinely. The urban freight operation is complex due to the fact that the UAV is likely to have to go both into integrated airspace (cruise) and low level (take-off and landing), so these UAVs must both integrate with ATM and U-Space. In both cases, flying above urban areas will be classified as a category C operation. A benefit of flying above urban areas is that manned aviation is not allowed near buildings, simplifying operations in terms of DAA for traffic. However, the density of infrastructures requires a DAA for fixed obstacles. Plus, these operations are likely to use stable flight routes, with deconfliction services required considering the operational risk. This asks for U-Space services from phase U3. Due to the size of these UAVs, and to reduce nuisance to the population, it is likely that some areas will be forbidden. Because of the large payloads, delivery from the air or dropping seems unlikely, so the freight UAV will have to land on some properly defined spaces. The limited amount of space will ask for rotorcrafts and/or possibly VTOL UAVs. Urban areas being well covered in terms of communication networks, ground communication will be the preferred solution.

Enabling these operations will take time, as there is no equivalent in manned aviation, so there is little experience.

Having a UAV transition from integrated airspace to low level will ask for equipage to deal with both environments. In integrated airspace, a DAA for traffic will be required, while in urban environment (take-off and landing) a DAA for obstacles will be needed. Developing both of these pieces of equipment for medium sized aircraft is a significant challenge and will ask for research to be done, especially on sensor miniaturization. The sensors will also be crucial for the localization part, as some urban areas can be GPS denied, asking for an independent localization mean. From a procedure point of view, insertion of a relatively slow UAV in the traffic will be challenging. At lower levels, dynamical flight planning will be needed to adapt to a future busy airspace around cities. Procedure for helipad use will also need to be defined, though this could benefit from regulations of cities with high helicopter traffic. A solution to the miniaturization problem can come from the automotive industry. Indeed, hardware and software developed for autonomous cars could answer the requirements for low level flight. The envisioned UAV being on a scale similar to cars, the Size Weight and Power (SWaP) requirements could match. From a procedure perspective, this type of operation will benefit from the advances brought by the current exploratory research projects on U-Space (see current SESAR2020 ERC projects). Alternatively, in the future, a drone could stay aloft and be used as a warehouse while being supplied by ground-to-air freight: Amazons floating warehouse [10].The idea is to have a medium altitude floating warehouse to which a swarm of drones have access. This might serve as a fast delivery platform, assuming the regulatory hurdles behind would be solved in the future. The company patented the design, with details about its fuel efficiency solutions for the route from airship to the delivery destination.

Freight related flights are likely to be among the first high impact operations to be enabled since they already exist and only require modifying the transport medium (from aircraft to UAV). Plus, they don't involve the transportation of humans, greatly reducing the risk. However, operations in urban areas will still ask for complex procedures and systems to be set up before they can take place.

B. Warehouses, Distribution Centers and Outlets Monitoring

Monitoring in those large buildings offers some challenges which can be eased with the help of drones. A wide range of applications can be envisioned like security protocol improvement, customer habits studies, process improvement, and inventorying [11]. Todays solutions can be expensive and lack efficiency. For example, inventory management of distribution centers is most of the time done by human workers via hand-held devices scanning through stocked pallets of goods in labyrinth like aisles. UASs abilities to move quickly and in 3-D will facilitate these tasks with an automated, flexible and cost-efficient solution. Fleets of UAVs going around a building with appropriate sensors can reduce the number of required sensors as well as their cost (closer range, so less costly). The autonomy level required for such tasks is to be able to navigate and avoid collisions with static obstacles and humans (assuming there are no other flying object). Automation will allow the routes to be changed dynamically by the operator providing flexibility and usage of a same fleet for different tasks. The fleet will operate for long periods of times with automated UAV replacement and charging. In this section, we limit ourselves to indoor operations. These applications don't ask for high speed, large payload or maneuverability, the main requirement will be endurance, plus it is indoors operations in a known environment subject to little perturbations. For such tasks, airships are the best pick as they provide high endurance and stability for onboard sensors. The two main tasks of navigation and collision avoidance ask for a precise localization system, which will most likely be based on Simultaneous Localization and Mapping (SLAM) methods which have been extensively studied. Existing sensors, even low-cost ones, like monocular cameras, would allow to perform this task. As there is no interaction with traffic, ATM, or U-Space, regulatory constraints will be low. The two main obstacles for this application are the high level of automation and the operation above the public, which asks for Category B regulatory requirements. Though it will not be the case for all applications, if the UASs operate above the public, they will require mitigation means to prevent any incident developing into injuries on ground. Again, airship provide some de-facto mitigation means because they are lighter than air. For the level of automation, operations with a pilot per UAV, or even one pilot for multiple UAV, does not seem like an economically viable solution. These applications will most likely ask for supervision only from one human who could perform other tasks.

Though not existing yet on the market, all the pieces for these applications are on the shelves. There are no strong regulatory or technological barriers to the introduction of UAS in this context.

C. Improving Customer Experience

According to 2018 retail predictions, the organizations have to review their structure to set the experience of the customers as their priority [12]. With the data based methods, such as machine learning, offering powerful solutions for customer data, it is easy to have a direct link to the habits of individuals which would help to offer preferable solutions to customers. This customer-centric approach would be likely to involve interaction between the customer and the organization both online and in stores, where a drone can be a part of this link. While the concerns of the public about drones is already on the rise before they have started to populate the sky, maybe indoors applications can serve as a warming environment to start with human-machine interactions. A scenario will be to have drone guides that will show you the path to the item of preference, saving time during the supermarket item searches. Their ability to move in 3-D already will allow them to point items in higher shelves where it might not be easy with other solutions. They can even calculate the best route to follow if a list of items is provided. They can offer alternatives for the missing items, shuffling through the database. Another possible application will be drones for assisting with car parking in malls. For big cities, finding a spot in a mall parking might be quite challenging. Multiple drones can work in harmony to guide the customers to the closest parking lot, and win the hearts of the public in time. Yet another application of drones might be to merge with virtual goggles, displaying the stream through a camera on the drone to wander in shops to see the items or environment without the need to actually be there. For example, this would help customers choose the less crowded time to go shopping, naturally improving the customer flow. In this type of application, two operations have to be distinguished: indoors and outdoors. As mentioned earlier, indoors operations are not concerned with civil aviation rules. However, contact with the public asks for risk mitigation measures. To reduce safety concerns, one solution could be to use very small drones (<800g). A rotorcraft or airship of this size would have sufficient autonomy to guide a customer while being small enough not to be a hazard. Since they will be flying in large aisles, avoiding obstacles is not a concern and avoiding the other drones will be the main challenge. Now, for the outdoor case, things get complicated. Mitigation measures to ensure that drones won't crash onto cars will be required. Indeed, a failure to the drone could lead to a car crash. The resulting risk is likely to classify this application in Category C. Moreover, at least U1 U-Space services will be required to ensure tracking and geocaging of the drones in the mall area. In both cases, the fleet management and autonomy aspects will be the main concerns, as they will determine the overall efficiency of the system. Human-machine interaction will also be crucial to allow easy communication between drones and customers. As far as guiding humans with drones is concerned, feasibility studies showed that drones can be used to guide blind runners [13]. Similarly, prototypes of flying street lights have been designed to guide people through cities[14]. Still, guiding simultaneously a group of persons is a challenge yet to be undertaken. For guiding cars, manufacturers like ford are currently exploring the solution for a wider application [15]; guiding cars through a parking could be a first step, yet a challenging one.

When it comes to customer experience, customers are used to have what they need, as they need it, at the time they want, most probably as fast as possible thanks to interactions with computers, internet and mobile networks. Thus, the companies are in a rush to keep up with the race of expectations, otherwise they face to lose the customers quite fast as well. Faster deliveries is of importance and how it might be achieved is described in the following section.

D. Delivery

As mentioned earlier, the advent of internet shopping has profoundly altered the logistics of retail. According to the BBC [16], parcel volumes surged almost 50% globally between 2014-2016 and they are on track to increase at rates of 17-28% annually up to 2021. This has bolstered the need to rethink logistics, particularly in the delivery part. Currently, delivery is mostly done with delivery vans and trucks. Because of the sheer volume of parcels, this is causing problems in big cities. According to [17], in Paris, one moving vehicle in five is a delivery vehicle, generating 25% of urban CO_2 emissions. Last mile delivery is also costly: it represents 20% of the cost of the whole delivery chain [18]. This is where drones may come in handy. With their low cost, automation, high speed and flexibility, they could become the future of delivery. This section focuses on the last leg of the journey, more specifically on the last mile delivery, between the warehouse and the customer or a pick-up point. This application can be declined in three operational scenarios: delivery to a remote location, to an urban pickup point, to a house or person in an urban area. Each of these scenarios has its own constraints that will be detailed in the following. For all applications, the main technological capacities needed are endurance, automation, maneuverability, payload carrying ability and DAA. The most important aspect is ensuring the integrity of the data used to automate the flight. If this data is corrupted then the flight might be jeopardized. This means several onboard sensors must be used and fused. Global Navigation Satellite System (GNSS) is to be avoided in the cities (too imprecise). And malicious corruption of the information source must be mitigated. Parcel delivery operations will likely fall within Category B. If parcel delivery falls outside of the set of pre-established specific scenarios, a risk analysis must be carried out and an authorization must be requested. Since delivery drones might be numerous, and certainly will not be the only drones in the urban sky, services from U-Space will need to be at least in phase U2.

1) To a remote location: This is the simplest scenario, flying to a remote location avoiding urban areas greatly reduces the risk to humans. This type of long range mission is best suited to fixed wing or VTOL UAV, with a connection through terrestrial or satellite network. Depending on the remote place to reach, flight can be performed at low levels, taking advantage of U-Space services, or at medium altitude which would require interactions with ATM, thus adding requirements on the operation. Assuming that the flight goes through low density air traffic, because of the remote location, constraints on DAA and deconfliction services are low. However, such long-range operations are likely to ask for a stable flight plan. Thus, a U-Space in phase U2 would be sufficient for this type of operation.

2) To a pickup point: Flying to a pickup point has various benefits. Firstly, the objective is fixed so a stable flight plan can be used. Secondly, a landing facility will be available at the pickup point. However, due to these operations being in urban areas, the landing facility is likely to be small, like a helipad, thus VTOL and rotorcraft will be the preferred UAVs. This type of operation will have to be integrated in the middle of a complex airspace above cities, asking for a U-Space in phase U2 to U3. Protection areas around cities will prevent interactions with manned aviation, so no interaction with ATM would be required in normal operations.

3) To a house/person: This is the most complex case, as each delivery has a different destination which can potentially move (moving person as target), asking for maneuverable aircraft like rotorcraft. From a procedural perspective, this asks for services capable of dynamic flight planning, dynamic geofencing and deconfliction to ensure that the drone is able to reach the person/house. Such a high level of dynamic airspace management asks for a U-Space in phase 4. On top of the equipage required to be integrated in the U-Space, the UAV will need to carry identification means to ensure that the parcel is delivered to the correct customer, increasing the payload. It is still unclear how delivery could be done: dropping the parcel would be dangerous for the customer, and the parcel; attaching it to a rope would jeopardize the flight and be dangerous to the population below; landing for the delivery would expose the drone to hazards like animals, or malicious humans.

As a summary, delivery drones must be agile, enduring, and loaded with sensors; this means that the maximum parcel weight they can carry might be reduced. This also means that the number of drones delivering parcels will be high; and since other drones will be flying for other missions (police, etc.) a high level of airspace management will be required, thus delaying the integration of these operations.

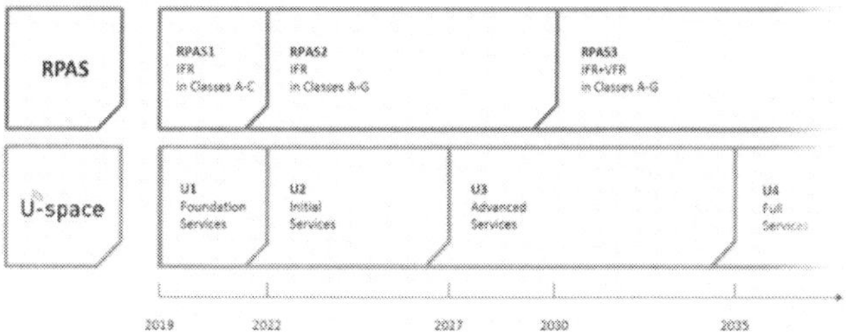

Figure 1. The European Union timelines for integration of drones with ATM (green), and with U-Space (orange).

E. *Advertisement*

Advertisement has evolved recently with the appearance of dynamic ads and recommender systems. Instead of advertising goods to an as large as possible audience, tailoring advertisement to the customer's needs is now possible. The integration of UASs is an opportunity to develop both approaches. For mass advertisement, UASs could be equipped with banners or signs, depending on their size. For targeted advertisement, displays on a UAV could allow displaying the relevant information to the right customer. For example, one could envision a delivery drone asking for the customer to watch an advertisement (just like on some web videos) before releasing the parcel. This would imply some design challenges. Indeed, UASs are systems optimized for a given operation, with all design factors: Cost, Size, Weight And Power (C-SWAP), being pushed to the limit. Any additional element not directly related to the mission or the UAS might jeopardize the optimality of the design. For example, adding advertisement structures would add significant aerodynamic drag asking for more power or a different structural design. Similarly, adding displays would increase the weight and require more power. This effect can be lessened by new technologies, e.g., by providing more powerful motors, more efficient batteries, better control laws. From a regulatory perspective, privacy concerns might arise from the fact that targeted advertisement in a public place can reveal personal information that a customer would prefer to keep private. This could be solved by technological means (e.g., displaying the advertisement on the customer's cellphone) but it could lead to more customer acceptability issues, on top of the ones linked to the presence of the advertisement itself. This type of operation could be started as soon as drone operations will be allowed in close proximity to humans.

This section presented the operational concepts related to each of the five considered applications, as well as the obstacles preventing their integration and existing projects. The next section compares the different obstacles with the timelines of large European efforts in order to forecast dates at which the required services and procedures will make the operation available.

IV. Enabling Timeline in Europe

Since the beginning, three types of obstacles have been considered for the integration of drones in various types of operations: technological, standardization and regulatory. In the European integration effort, each of these locks is currently tackled by an international effort. Technological locks are being identified and dealt with by SESAR2020, the coordination body for ATM research and development. Lack of standardization is addressed by EUROCAE, the main aeronautical standardisation body in Europe, especially the working group WG-105 dedicated to UAS. In terms of regulation, the EASA is developing a regulation for drone operations.

In terms of obstacles, it appears from the analysis of the previous operations that the biggest obstacles when introducing UAS are likely to be:

- Safety aspects, especially related to the presence of humans near the operation,
- The need to integrate with ATM, or U-Space services, or both,
- High automation levels,
- Definition of standards for UAS sub-systems.

The obstacles and ongoing efforts deployed in Europe are presented side-by-side for each type of operation in Table II.

When the humans are involved in the operation, the risk is lower, and in fact such a scenario is on its way to being regulated in some countries. For this reason, drones for monitoring in non-public places are already at hand. Now when the humans are not part of the operations, like in the customers monitoring and customer assistance operations, mitigation factors are required to ensure a low overall risk level. For both applications, the UAV design and size can be chosen to provide safe operation (e.g., UAV in a ball, micro UAV). For flights far from humans and traffic, the complexity of the operation is related to the amount of interactions with the rest of the traffic. Operating in the middle of a dense traffic is a lot more complex than in less occupied airspaces. For this reason, delivery to remote places will likely come fairly soon. The second obstacle is interactions with the ATM system and manned traffic, though this is a highly complex problem, the fact that it is being actively investigated will enable these operations, like cargo drones, relatively soon. Now, another factor that may delay some operations is the automation level. Indeed, the regulation being developed envisions a pilot for each UAV in Category C operations and possibly one pilot for multiple UAVs for Category B operations. However, to be feasible, some operations will require full autonomy with little or no supervision. We believe this level of acceptance and trust will come only after years of successful drone operations, at which point offering drone services for customer experience outdoors will become a realistic application. Finally, the integration of UAS in high traffic density airspaces, like the future airspace above cities, asks for numerous mitigation measures that large UAV (e.g., freight UAV) will be able to carry, allowing them to operate earlier than smaller ones. Small UAV operations, like parcel delivery, will come with the miniaturization of equipment and setup of UAS traffic management, but that will ask for time.

Based on the SESAR-JU roadmap for integration of drones in ATM and EASA's U-Space roll-out (see Figure 1), considering that EASA regulation is planned for 2019, and in view of EUROCAE's ongoing work, we propose tentative dates for the beginning of each operation. For the EUROCAE timeline, currently studied topics (DAA traffic, C2 link, ATOL) are expected to yield standards in three years (around 2021). Topics not studied yet, if started this year, would still take four to five years to complete. Note that these dates represent the

TABLE II. OPERATION TYPES, MAIN OBSTACLES TO INTEGRATION, CURRENT EFFORTS TO SOLVE THEM, AND TENTATIVE DATES FOR INTEGRATION IN THE EUROPEAN CIVIL AVIATION CONTEXT.

Application	Main obstacles	Main ongoing efforts from civil aviation communities	Prospective beginning date
Freight			
LUCA	ATM integration, C2 link, DAA traffic, ATOL	SESAR2020 projects for RPAS, EUROCAE WG-105 developing standards (DAA, C2link, ATOL).	2022
Urban	ATM integration, U-Space U2 deployment, DAA obstacles, safety (Cat. C)	SESAR2020 projects for RPAS, SESAR2020 projects for U-SPACE, automotive sector developing sensors, existing helicopter procedures.	2027
Monitoring			
Public	High level of automation, public safety	Not regulated by civil aviation authorities.	2018
No public	High level of automation	Not regulated by civil aviation authorities.	2018
Guide			
Indoors	High level of automation, public acceptance	Not regulated by civil aviation authorities.	2018
Outdoors	High level of automation, public acceptance, U-Space U1 deployment, safety (Cat C.)	SESAR2020 projects for U-SPACE, EASA's regulatory framework	2022-2023
Delivery			
to remote location	ATM integration, U-Space U2 deployment, C2 link, DAA traffic, safety (Cat B.)	SESAR2020 projects for RPAS, SESAR2020 projects for U-SPACE, EUROCAE WG-105 developing standards (DAA, C2link).	2022
to pickup point	U-Space U3 deployment, safety (Cat B.)	SESAR2020 projects for U-SPACE, EASA's regulatory framework	2027
to house/person	U-Space U4 deployment, safety (Cat B.)	SESAR2020 projects for U-SPACE, EASA's regulatory framework	2035
Advertisement	Public acceptance	Not regulated by civil aviation authorities.	2018

times at which integration will be possible, however it does not ensure that the industry will develop the applications and that the public will be ready to accept them.

V. CONCLUSION

This paper presented five envisioned applications, with associated operations for UAS, that will impact the retail sector. Each type of operation has been described, and enabling technologies, standards, rules and services have been put forward. This allowed to provide an estimation as to when the different operations will become possible. One must remain careful regarding these estimations as the retail habits are very different from one country to another, and some countries may want to push some applications regardless of the difficulties. The same applies for regulation, with some countries going faster and being more liberal.

REFERENCES

[1] B. Smith and G. Linden, "Two decades of recommender systems at amazon.com," IEEE Internet Computing, vol. 21, no. 3, May-June 2017, pp. 12–18. [Online]. Available: doi.ieeecomputersociety.org/10.1109/MIC.2017.72

[2] Reuters. French retailers in Drive to win market share. URL: https://www.reuters.com/article/france-retail-drive/french-retailers-in-drive-to-win-market-share-idUSL6E8INECL20120724, [retrieved: 04, 2018]. (2012)

[3] Econsultancy. Fashion ecommerce: are virtual fitting rooms the silver bullet? URL: https://www.econsultancy.com/blog/66058-fashion-ecommerce-are-virtual-fitting-rooms-the-silver-bullet, [retrieved: 04, 2018]. (2015)

[4] P. R. Wurman, R. D'Andrea, and M. Mountz, "Coordinating hundreds of cooperative, autonomous vehicles in warehouses," AI magazine, vol. 29, no. 1, 2008, p. 9.

[5] Softbankrobotics. Who is Pepper? URL: https://www.ald.softbankrobotics.com/en/robots/pepper, [retrieved: 04, 2018]. (2018)

[6] Amazon. Amazon Prime Air. URL: https://www.amazon.com/Amazon-Prime-Air/b?ie=UTF8&node=8037720011, [retrieved: 04, 2018]. (2018)

[7] SESAR-JU. U-Space blueprint. URL: https://www.sesarju.eu/u-space-blueprint, [retrieved: 04, 2018]. (2017)

[8] M. P. Collins, "The future market for large unmanned cargo aircraft in the national airspace system," Ph.D. dissertation, Lewis University, 2017.

[9] SESAR-JU. SESAR2020: PJ10-05. URL: https://www.atmmasterplan.eu/data/sesar_solutions/347, [retrieved: 04, 2018]. (2017)

[10] Telegraph. Amazon's flying warehouses to dispatch drone deliveries from the sky. URL: http://www.telegraph.co.uk/technology/2016/12/29/amazons-flying-warehouses-dispatch-drone-deliveries-sky/, [retrieved: 04, 2018]. (2016)

[11] Overflo. How Drones Are Changing the Face of Warehousing. URL: http://www.overflo.com/blog/drone-delivery.html, [retrieved: 04, 2018]. (2016)

[12] InternetRetailing. 2018 Retail predictions. From drones to the changing customer experience. URL: http://internetretailing.net/2018/01/customer-experience/, [retrieved: 04, 2018]. (2018)

[13] M. Al Zayer, S. Tregillus, J. Bhandari, D. Feil-Seifer, and E. Folmer, "Exploring the use of a drone to guide blind runners," in Proceedings of the 18th International ACM SIGACCESS Conference on Computers and Accessibility. ACM, 2016, pp. 263–264.

[14] DesignBoom. Fleetlights: a prototype team of flying torch drones to guide the way at night. URL: https://www.designboom.com/technology/fleetlights-direct-line-drone-app-11-18-2016/, [retrieved: 04, 2018]. (2016)

[15] IndustryWeek. Ford Studies Drone Use to Guide Self-Driving Cars. URL: http://www.industryweek.com/automation/ford-studies-drone-use-guide-self-driving-cars, [retrieved: 04, 2018]. (2016)

[16] BBC. Crowded streets: Cities face a surge in online deliveries. URL: http://www.bbc.com/news/business-42245367, [retrieved: 04, 2018]. (2018)

[17] RungisInternational. Transport, la logistique du dernier kilometre (Transports, the logistics of the last mile). URL: https://www.rungisinternational.com/a-l-heure-du-digital/transport-logistique-dernier-kilometre/, [retrieved: 04, 2018]. (2017)

[18] TechnologyReview. Urban Drone Deliveries Are Finally Taking Flight. URL: https://www.technologyreview.com/the-download/608912/urban-drone-deliveries-are-finally-taking-flight/, [retrieved: 04, 2018]. (2017)

Digital Management of Multiple Advertising Displays

Arménio Baptista, Alina Trifan, António Neves
DETI/IEETA
Universidade de Aveiro
Aveiro, 3810-193

{armenio, alina.trifan, an}@ua.pt

Abstract—**The technological boom that we have been experiencing in the last decade has impacted the retail sector in many ways. Captivating customers through smart advertising, engaging them in the retail process and enhancing their experience has been a long-time desideratum in this industry. Recent technology makes it possible to follow unprecedented approaches for achieving these goals. In this paper, we present a strategy based on a series of autonomous stations (either static, such as monitors, or mobile, such as autonomous robots) that can be used in any type of multimedia advertising across one or multiple entities. We present preliminary developments of this concept in an attempt to impact modern advertising. As a final product, this project aims to produce an autonomous system capable of displaying multimedia contents across several monitors.**

Keywords–Advertising; Cloud-based platform, Digital Contents Management; Multimedia.

I. INTRODUCTION

One of the keys to the success of the retail industry passes by advertising to the general public, mainly by using marketing strategies [1]. The technological evolution, more and more, has an important role in the marketing and the advertise of products [2]. In [3], experimental results show that sales in hypermarkets are enhanced when digital displays are used.

The main focus of this paper is to propose a solution to control the multimedia resources and display them using a unique platform which provides the management and manipulation over the resources in order to produce a final content to better fit the monitor associated to a terminal. This solution allows the control, maintenance, composition and division of the multimedia resources across the stations, displaying the information that the user selects into the different terminals. It also proposes a solution to control the permissions to the resources for each user logged in the platform. In order to handle the multimedia files uploaded by the users, the solution proposes the use of the FFmpeg library [4], which has compatibility with all major formats and codecs.

As it is a project in development, there are much aspects to improve and features to add. However, this paper exposes all the decisions made until date, starting with a system overview, following the management of the multimedia resources and the users and finally some preliminary results. This paper is structured in three other sections.

Section II overviews the methods that we followed in implementing this system. We present preliminary results in Section III and we assess the importance of this work and discuss future work directions in Section IV.

II. METHODOLOGY

The main goal of this project is to design a system capable to store, manipulate and manage multimedia contents uploaded by the users. This involves three major agents: the Web server, the control dashboard and the monitors, resulting in an architecture, as presented in Figure 1.

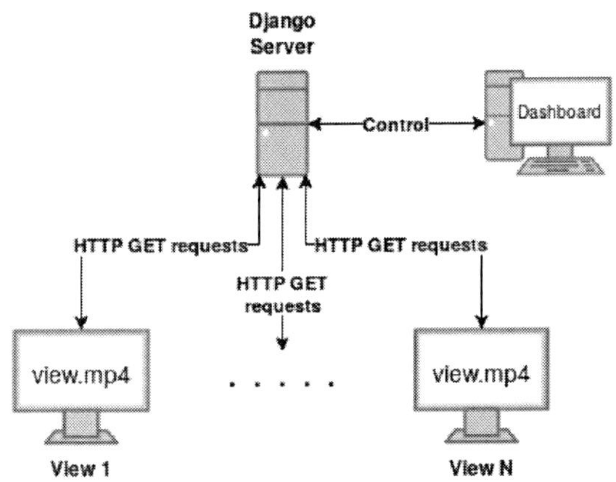

Figure 1. Proposed system architecture.

This architecture allows the Web server to control all the monitors (using HTTP requests to communicate) and expose a Web site so the users can manage them. Making the Web server a unique point of communication, the synchronization of the updates made by the users and the monitors is immediate.

A. *Resources division*

In order to split and organize the multimedia resources, a solution of three components is proposed, as described in Figure 2:

- **Contents:** base element of the multimedia resources, which is basically an image or video uploaded by the users.
- **Timelines:** set of Contents with a predefined sequence, much similar to a video composed of different contents. If the Content is an image, the user may define the duration of the image to be shown in the Timeline.
- **Views:** set of Timelines with a predefined sequence that is associated to a physical terminal. The final product to be displayed on the monitor and the only

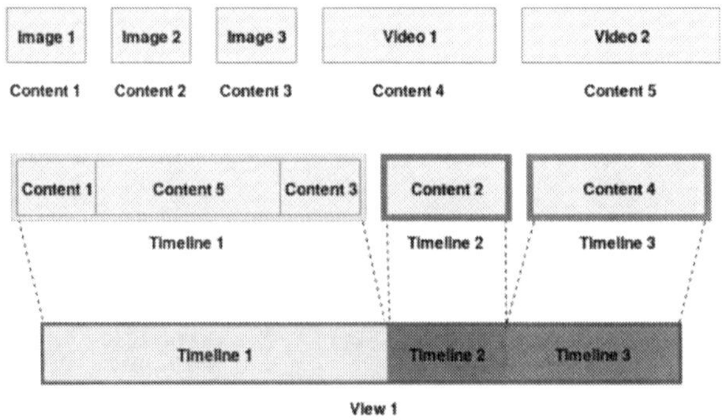

Figure 2. Resources composition.

way to create a View is with the connection of a terminal.

This division between the resources gives freedom to the users to create and dispose multimedia contents into any order and consequently display them. It also allows the users to reuse the Timelines in different Views without the need to recreate them again.

B. Users

In order to restrict the improper access of the users to the multimedia resources, a login system is proposed with different credentials and permission levels of the users. Therefore, before accessing the control dashboard, the system asks for the login credentials of the user. Django [5] has an user authentication system, which facilitates the implementation.

To control the users, the system has an *administrator superuser* that has access to a section in the dashboard that allows the management of the users (creation, edition, deletion and permissions). Then, the system has two types of users:

- **Administrator:** user responsible to manage the users access to the dashboard and their permissions for each resource. Additionally, the manager can add, edit and delete any resource, having no restrictions for his actions.
- **Regular User:** user with permissions predefined by the administrator and only with access to the resources predefined by those permissions.

C. Permissions

Given a scenario where the system is deployed in a shared environment between different users and the discretion of the resources needs to be maintained in order to block the modification of resources not owned by that user, a solution of permissions with two levels is proposed:

1) Resource level: The resource level has three different types of permissions: Contents, Timelines and Views. This permission defines what resources the user can create and edit and only the allowed ones will be displayed in the interface of the corresponding user.

2) Object level: The object level is basically what resources the user can access. By default, the user only has access to the resources he has created, although, the administrator can give access to a certain resource to a user.

The users with Timelines and Views permissions can view all the underlying resources in order to create a Timeline or View. To create a View, the user can use any of the underlying Timelines and to create a Timeline, the user can use any of the underlying Contents.

These blocking permissions allow, not only the creation of users to a specific task, but also provide the cooperation of users to a final multimedia product. As an example of specific tasks we can think of giving Content and Timeline permissions (Resource level) to a designer responsible to provide multimedia contents to the system or giving View permissions to a user responsible to the monitors inside of a specific building.

D. Website - control dashboard

In order to facilitate the control over the system, a website using the Django web framework was created. This dashboard gives control over four main resources: Contents, Timelines, Views and Users. Only the users with permissions over the resources can access and control the respective resource and only the administrator can edit these permissions and have access to the Users page. However, a regular user can edit his/her own profile information.

E. Image and video handling

Developing a system that handles multimedia contents needs the proper handling of the uploaded files. The system supports two types of files:

- **Image:** JPEG [6], PNG [7] among other image file formats supported by ffmpeg.
- **Video:** AVI and MP4 video file formats, among other video/audio containers supported by ffmpeg. All the video codecs supported by ffmpeg can be used (ex. H.264 [8], H.265 [9], just to name a few).

The upload of the files is made with the File Upload of Django and saved in a media directory of the server.

1) View creation: Upon the configuration of a View, if it has Timelines associated, the server begins the process to create the MP4 file associated to the view. This file is compressed using the H.264 standard [8], encoded with YUV420 at 25 frames per second, as all subjacent videos of the Timeline.

To better fit the resolution associated to the monitor, all the Contents are adapted to this resolution. In other words, when a View is configured with Timelines associated, the system goes through all the Contents associated to these Timelines and makes the changes needed to fit the screen resolution.

To create, manipulate and merge these files, the FFmpeg library was chosen since it has compatibility with all major video and image formats. The FFmpeg library adapts the Contents using mostly padding and resize transformations. When iterating over the frames of the Contents, the FFmpeg library resizes the frames which have different size from the resolution and applies padding to keep the Contents aspect ratio.

F. Connecting a monitor

The interaction between the different terminals (a single board like a Raspberry PI [10] and a monitor) and the Django server is made with HTTP requests from a terminal. In order

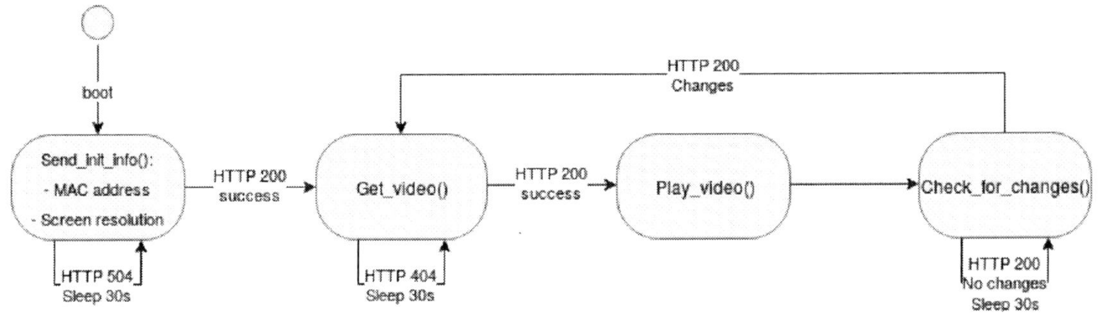

Figure 3. Monitor lifecycle.

to do this, a Python script was created and is responsible to control the terminal and its lifecycle (see Figure 3). When the terminal starts, the script runs on boot and goes through a series of steps in order to register in the server (if it is the first time connecting) and download the video.

Firstly, the terminal sends a HTTP POST request method with some information of his own:

- **MAC address:** this information allows the server to distinguish the different terminals and allows the user to know which View is associated to a terminal.
- **Screen resolution:** the resolution is used by the server to adapt the Contents associated with some View to its screen resolution.

The server, receiving this information, checks if the MAC address already exists and returns the path in the server to the video corresponding to that View.

Secondly, the terminal tries to download the video from the server with a HTTP GET request. If it fails (if the View wasnt configured yet or the server is down), the terminal waits a short time, thirty seconds by default, and tries to download it again. This loop is repeated until the video successfully downloads.

Finally, the video is played in loop and the terminal enters in a loop which keeps sending HTTP GET requests (with a time interval) to the server to check for changes in the video. This polling requests ensure if changes are detected, the video being displayed in the monitor is updated.

III. Results

While the work presented in this paper is a project in development, preliminary results regarding the current stage of development are presented in this section in order to confirm the effectiveness of the system.

A. Dashboard

As noticeable in Figure 5, the dashboard has a top Navigation bar, which has a Dropdown button so the user can edit his personal informations or logout, and a left Navigation bar with four possible navigations. This left Navigation bar only shows the possible navigations to which the user has access. When accessing a resource from the left Navigation bar, one of the pages presented in Figure 5 (except User) is displayed. This page allows the visualization over the existing Contents, Timelines or Views that the user has access. It also allows to create (except for Views as explained in Section II-F), edit or delete a resource and, if the user is the administrator, to edit the permissions (object level) of the users to that resource.

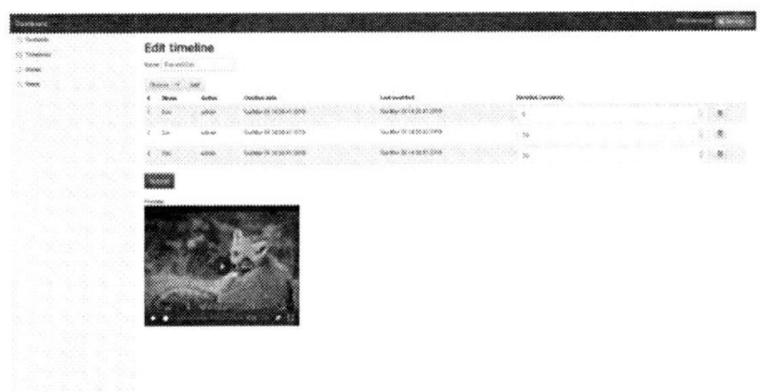

Figure 4. Edition of a created Timeline.

When editing a resource, a form is displayed so the user can edit the data associated to that resource, as shown in Figure 4. In the case of Contents, the name can be edited and a file upload button allows a new upload. However, when editing a Timeline or a View, a table with the Contents or Timelines associated to the resource, respectively, is displayed. This table allows the addition of objects from the dropdown button. Moreover, the objects from the table can be dragged and dropped into the intended order. When editing a Timeline, the table also has a duration input field for each image object. By filling in this field the user can specify the intended duration of each image that will be part of the timeline. In addition, a preview window displaying the video reproduced from the last Timeline submission is available.

B. Permissions

The platform that we propose supports user permissions at two distinct levels. On one hand, at the level of the resources and on the other hand, at the level of the objects. The administrator manages these permissions through the graphical interface as we will describe next.

1) Resource level: When creating a user, the administrator fills a form with some information associated to the user as in Figure 6. Note that this form has three Checkbox fields, each one for a resource (Content, Timeline and View). These Checkboxes are the permissions at resource level of the user being created and will define which resources the user will have access in the left Navigation bar.

Figure 5. Visualization of Contents, Timelines and Views.

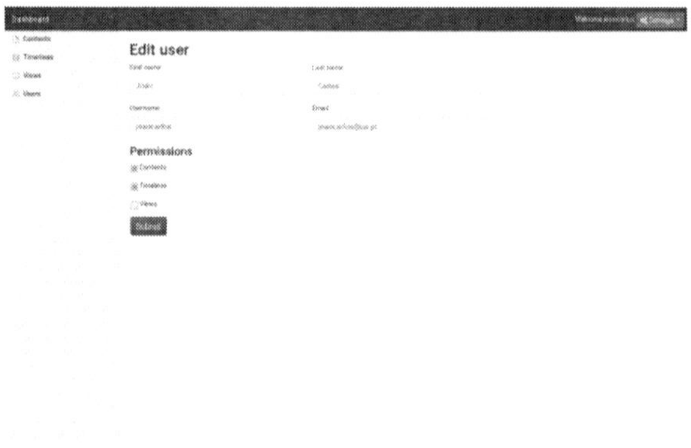

Figure 6. User edition with resource level permissions.

2) Object level: In Figure 5, there is a padlock for each object of the table. This padlock redirects to a page where the administrator edits the permissions over the respective object, as in Figure 7. This page lists all users with resource level permission over the resource of the object, so the administrator can grant access to that object.

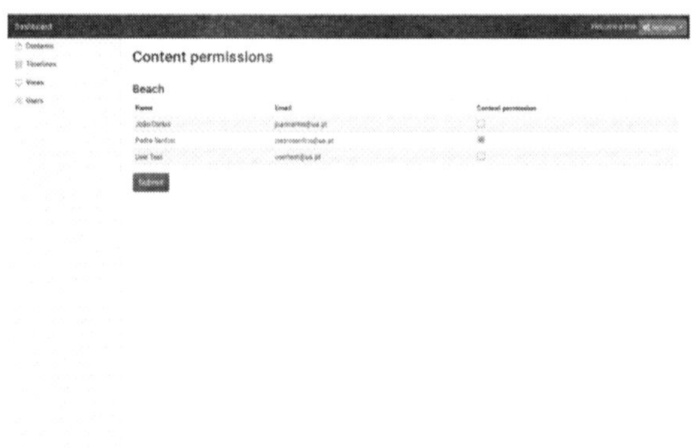

Figure 7. Modification of object level permissions of a Content.

C. Multimedia contents transformation

In Figure 8, it is possible to verify the transformations of FFmpeg. The figure shows five frames of a Timeline with three Contents (an image, a video and another image) with these resolutions:

- Image 1: 1000x665 px
- Video: 1280x720 px
- Image 2: 6000x1977 px

Before explaining the FFmpeg transformations to these 5 frames, it is important to refer 3 effects: letterboxing, pillarboxing and windowboxing [11]. Letterboxing consists in the transformation of frames with widescreen aspect ratio (16:9) to a standard-width video ratio (4:3) while preserving the frames original aspect ratio. This transformation consists of a padding transformation both on top and bottom of the frames.

On the contrary, the pillarboxing effect, consists in the transformation of a standard-width video format into a widescreen aspect ratio by applying padding into the frames both on left and right.

Windowboxing consists of the combination of both effects: letterboxing and pillarboxing. This is noticeable when the frames of a video are centered in the screen with a padding effect all around them. This happens when the resolution of the screen is bigger than the frames and no resize transformation is used.

Using FFmpeg with the arguments:

- "scale" and "force_original_aspect_ratio"
- "pad"

makes it is possible to apply the intended transformations to the frames.

The "scale" parameter allows to specify the scale resolution to apply into the frames, while using the "force_original_aspect_ratio" to maintain the original aspect ratio of the images. This transformation will upscale the frames, if the resolution of the screen is bigger than the frames, and downscale, in the opposite situation. The "pad" parameter allows to apply padding to the frames after the scale transformation. When the frames of the Contents have a different aspect ratio of the screen, the letterboxing and pillarboxing are perceptible.

Back to Figure 8, the example uses the FFmpeg to fit a monitor with a 1366x768 resolution which has a 1.78:1 aspect ratio. In Image 1 from Figure 8, as the resolution of the image is smaller than the screen, FFmpeg resizes the frames using an upscaling transformation to fit the screen. Although, as the aspect ratio of the image (1.5:1) is smaller than the screen (1.78:1), FFmpeg also applies a padding effect, resulting in a pillarboxing effect.

In the Video from Figure 8, FFmpeg resizes the frames using an upscaling transformation. In this case, the aspect ratio of the frames (1.78:1) and the screen (1.78:1) are equal, so

Figure 8. Expansion of a Timeline with five frames from three Contents (Image 1 (fox), Video (tree frames) and Image 2 (mountain landscape).

FFmpeg doesn't apply the padding effect and the frames fit perfectly the screen.

Image 2 from Figure 8 is exactly the opposite of Image 1. The resolution of the frames is much bigger than the screen and FFmpeg resizes the frames, but using a downscale transformation. As for the padding effect, the frames of the image (3:1) have a much bigger aspect ratio than the screen (1.78:1), so FFmpeg applies padding to the frames, resulting in a letterboxing effect.

With these FFmpeg arguments, the result will never reach a windowboxing effect, because the "scale" parameter will always try to resize the frames to fit the screen and the "pad" parameter will compensate the difference between the aspect ratios, either with letterboxing or pillarboxing effects. Using the FFmpeg upscaling transformation over the frames of the Contents may have influence in the final quality of the frames if the resolution of the image is much smaller than the screen, which forces the users to upload Contents with an appropriate resolution.

D. Final result

Figure 9. Monitor displaying a video using a Raspberry Pi to communicate with the system.

In Figure 9, we can see a real Full HD monitor (1920x1080 px of resolution and a 1.78:1 aspect ratio) with a Raspberry PI single board connected to the developed system displaying the final output, the video stream for that View.

IV. Conclusion

The main goal of this paper was to propose a solution to manage multiple multimedia contents in order to display them in multiple monitors. The system we have presented, as a whole, is operational and ready to manage the upload of multimedia contents and display them. It implies the existence of a computer to host the server (with proper image and video processing capability), monitors to display the contents, single boards to connect to the monitor (like a Raspberry Pi) and, of course, network connection between the server and the terminals.

A global overview over the results, highlights some features that we intend to improve, as future work. Such features are:

- The aspect of the dashboard that needs to be more appealing and intuitive to the user and display for example, snapshots of the Contents;
- A more advanced Timeline editor in order to give the user a greater control over the sequence of Contents;
- The capability to fetch information in real time about the monitor in order to show the status in the dashboard; Moreover, making it possible to run certain commands over the monitor, like turn on and turnoff would be a desired improvement of this work.

In the future, as the system improves, we intend to expand the supported formats of Contents, like supporting some presentation formats (PDF or PowerPoint), as well as audio files. This enhancement of the system would eventually imply a reformulation of Timelines creation in the dashboard. Another interesting feature that we plan to develop is the support for the interaction between the target audience and the system, either by a physical contact or even by voice control. This interaction would allow the user to pause and skip contents, for example.

While this is still a project in development, the preliminary results are optimistic and encourage us to improve the current solution by extending several of its features, as detailed.

Acknowledgment

This work was partially funded by FEDER (Programa Operacional Factores de Competitividade - COMPETE) and by National Funds through the FCT - Foundation for Science and Technology in the context of the project UID/CEC/00127/2013.

References

[1] A. Di Rienzo, F. Garzotto, P. Cremonesi, C. Frà, and M. Valla, "Towards a smart retail environment," in *Adjunct Proceedings of the 2015 ACM International Joint Conference on Pervasive and Ubiquitous Computing and Proceedings of the 2015 ACM International Symposium on Wearable Computers*. ACM, 2015, pp. 779–782.

[2] N. I. Bruce, B. Murthi, and R. C. Rao, "A dynamic model for digital advertising: The effects of creative format, message content, and targeting on engagement," *Journal of Marketing Research*, vol. 54, no. 2, pp. 202–218, 2017.

[3] A. L. Roggeveen, J. Nordfält, and D. Grewal, "Do digital displays enhance sales? role of retail format and message content," *Journal of Retailing*, vol. 92, no. 1, pp. 122–131, 2016.

[4] "FFmpeg," http://ffmpeg.org/, accessed: 2018-04-18.

[5] "Django," https://djangoproject.com, accessed: 2018-04-18.

[6] G. K. Wallace, "The jpeg still picture compression standard," *IEEE transactions on consumer electronics*, vol. 38, no. 1, pp. xviii–xxxiv, 1992.

[7] C. Wilbur, "Png: The definitive guide," *Journal of Computing in Higher Education*, vol. 12, no. 2, pp. 94–97, 2001.

[8] T. Wiegand, G. J. Sullivan, G. Bjontegaard, and A. Luthra, "Overview of the h. 264/avc video coding standard," *IEEE Transactions on circuits and systems for video technology*, vol. 13, no. 7, pp. 560–576, 2003.

[9] V. Sze, M. Budagavi, and G. J. Sullivan, "High efficiency video coding (hevc)," *Integrated Circuit and Systems, Algorithms and Architectures. Springer*, vol. 39, p. 40, 2014.

[10] "Raspberry PI," https://www.raspberrypi.org/, accessed: 2018-04-18.

[11] C. Poynton, *Digital video and HD: Algorithms and Interfaces*. Elsevier, 2012.

Application of Multi-Agent Reinforcement Learning Techniques in Sequential Games

Vanya Markova, Ventseslav Shopov

Institute of Robotics
Bulgarian Academy of Sciences
Plovdiv
Bulgaria
Email: markovavanya@yahoo.com, vkshopov@yahoo.com

Abstract—**This article focuses on the application of multi-agent deep reinforcement learning techniques in sequential games. The main hypothesis is that deep reinforcement learning and collective behaviour approach demonstrate better performance than classic reinforcement learning. So autonomous agents are capable of discovering good solutions to the problem at hand by cooperate with other learners.**

Index Terms—**autonomous agents; deep reinforcement learning; multi-agent systems; collective behaviour**

I. Introduction

We employ deep multi-agent reinforcement learning to model the emergence of cooperation. The new notion of sequential social dilemmas allows us to model how rational agents interact, and arrive at more or less cooperative behaviours depending on the nature of the environment and the agents cognitive capacity. The research may enable us to better understand and control the behaviour of complex multi-agent systems.

The mathematical framework for question of unsupervised learning and autonomous decision making: is Reinforcement Learning (RL). In RL, a software agent interacts with an environment and occasionally perceives rewards to learn an optimal behavioural policy. Deep reinforcement learning combines established reinforcement learning techniques with the ability of deep neural networks to capture structure in complex environments and generalize over large state spaces. While deep reinforcement learning is still in its infancy, researchers and practitioners are rapidly exploring new applications. We want to develop this framework in sequential decision making in game theory. The aim of this paper is to apply this techniques of Multi-Agent Reinforcement Learning (MARL) and Multi-Agent Deep Reinforcement Learning (MADRL) and evaluate results of process of learning in sequential games. In real life, cooperating require complex behaviours, involving difficult sequences of actions that agents need to learn to execute by deep multi-agent reinforcement learning [1] [2].

Since the work on learning ATARI TV games by Google DeepMind [3], end-to-end reinforcement learning or deep reinforcement learning is garnering attention. This approach extends reinforcement learning to the entire process from sensors to motors by forming it using an artificial neural network especially a deep network without designing state space or action space explicitly [4]–[6].

Pursuit-evasion is a problem area in computer science in which one group of agents attempts to catch members of another group in an environment [7]. The reinforcement learning techniques have been used in some of recent studies in the field of pursuit-evasion games [8] [7]. A survey of actor-critic reinforcement learning is given in [9].

Sequential decision making under uncertainty is always a challenge for autonomous agents populating a multi-agent environment, since their behaviour is inevitably influenced by the behaviour of others. Further, agents have to constantly struggle to find the right balance between exploiting current information regarding the environment and the rest of its inhabitants, and exploring so that they acquire additional information. Moreover, they need to profitably trade off short-term rewards with anticipated long-term ones, while learning through interaction about the environment and others, employing techniques from RL, a fundamental area of study within Artificial Intelligence (AI) [10]–[13].

Coalition formation is a problem of great interest within game theory and AI, allowing autonomous individually rational agents to form stable or transient teams (or coalitions) to tackle an underlying task. Agents participating in realistic scenarios of repeated coalition formation need to successfully negotiate the terms of their participation in coalitions often having to compromise individual with team welfare effectively [14].

In our work, we assume that the environment dynamics or the types (capabilities) of other agents are not known, and thus the agents have to account for this uncertainty, in a Bayesian way [2], when making decisions. Handling type uncertainty allows information about others acquired within one setting to be exploited in possibly different settings in the future. The core of our contributions lies in the area of coalition formation under uncertainty. We studied several aspects of both the cooperative and non-cooperative facets of this problem, coining new theoretical concepts, proving theoretical results, presenting and evaluating algorithms for use in this context, and proposing a Bayesian RL framework for repeated coalition formation under uncertainty.

An essential quality of a cognitive being is its ability to learn, that is, to gain new knowledge or skills, as well as to improve existing knowledge or skills based on experience. Cognitive beings are able to cope with situations they have been previously confronted with as well as they are able to adapt to new situations sensibly. Thus, when designing an artificial agent that shall exhibit cognitive qualitieswhich we refer to in short as a cognitive agentone central task is to develop computational means that enable the agent to learn. In this paper, we subscribe to one of the most influential paradigms of machine learning, reinforcement learning (RL) [15]. Reinforcement learning is very valuable when the characteristics of the underlying system are not known and/or difficult to describe or when the environment of an acting agent is only partially known or completely unknown.

In recent years, there are many application of reinforcement learning techniques in multi-agent systems. There are a representative selection of algorithms for the different areas of multi-agent reinforcement learning research [2] [16].

Agents situated in the real world can perceive a great variety of information. Two situations are unlikely to lead to the same perception even if the situations are very similar. Learning requires the agent to acknowledge important details in a perception, to recognise commonalities across situations, and, most importantly, to disregard irrelevant information. In other words, the ability to learn involves the ability to abstract. Abstraction enables us to conceptualise the surrounding world, to build categories, and to derive reactions from these categories that can adapt to different situations. Complex and overly detailed circumstances can be reduced to much simpler concepts and not until then it becomes feasible to deliberate about conclusions to draw and actions to take. Abstract concepts explicate commonalities in different scenes and, thus, can cover new situations [17]–[21].

The question of how the solution, inferred by RL can be used to enable the cognitive agent to adapt the behavior to new tasks or similar situations is a great challenge in engineering machine learning. For this kind of reuse of knowledge, the term transfer training has become popular [22].

The main goal of this paper is to apply transfer learning trough reinforcement learning in area of building autonomous agent behaviour. In the second part of this paper we will briefly describe the underlying theory of Autonomous Agent, Markov Decision Process, Reinforcement Learning, Transfer Learning, Deep Learning and Sequential Games. In addition, we will describe the implementation of our approach. In the third part of our study we describe the experiments and gathers evidence to support our hypothesis.

II. Methods and Materials

A. Theory

1) Autonomous Agent behaviour: The information about past and current states of the agent and environment allow the agents to estimate its own progress. Moreover, this information allow the agent to make the corrections in existing pans if any needed and even to ma make new plans if it is necessary.

However if the agent makes corrections in the existing plans too often then this could lead to poor overall performance. Moreover, the frequently dropping and building plans could make the things even worse. Hence, it is desirable to reduce (or completely avoid) situations in which the agent should changes its mind. There are two main approaches to do that: the first is to make the changing of the plans less recourse consuming task and the e second is to make such plans that are able to deal with volatile environment behaviour. This material is concerning the second approach.

As a key issue in building more efficient plans in rapidly changing environment we can point the ability of the agent to makes its plans in accordance not only with past and current states of the environment but also bearing in mind the future. To do that the agent needs to predict or forecast the future states of the environment. So, if we describe the states of the agent and environment as a time series then the task of making efficient plans will be significantly aided if the agent could forecasts the future with desirable accuracy.

An n-tipple (vector) is a result of one cycle of a work of the agent. It consists of the parameters of the behaviour of the agent: $b(b1, b2, \dots, bn)$. The data from environment are collected and transformed into time series in the knowledge base of the agent.

2) Markov Decision Process: We formulate the transfer learning problem in sequential decision making domains using the following framework of Markov Decision Process. We use the following definition of MDP as a 5-tuple

$$< S, A, P, R, \gamma > \quad (1)$$

where the set of states, set of actions, transition function and reward function are described. And

$$P : S \times A \rightarrow \Pi(S) \quad (2)$$

is a transition function that maps the probability of moving to a new state given an action and the current state,

$$R : S \times A \rightarrow R \quad (3)$$

is a reward function. that gives the immediate reward of taking an action in a state.

And

$$\gamma \in [0, 1) \quad (4)$$

is the discount factor.

So, the MDP of the agent is described in (1), where S is the set of states, A is the set of actions, P is transition function and R is a reward function. The transition function P maps the the probability of moving to a new state given an action and the current states is shown in (2). The reward functions R that gives the immediate reward of taking an action is described in (3). An the discount factor γ is bounded as is shown in (4).

3) Reinforcement learning: Reinforcement learning [15] is a popular and effective method to solve an MDP.

In our work we implement the reinforcement learning algorithm Q-learning as is described in [23]. At each moment of time, the agent is in a given state $s \in S$, and the agents view is represented by a feature vector. Upon this information the agent makes the decision which action a from a set of all possible actions A to take in order to reach its goal. The outcome of Q-learning is a Q-function

$$Q(s, a) \tag{5}$$

that attaches to any state-action tuple (s, a) the expected reward over time. We discuss here the overall reward when starting in s and executing action a. From that Q-function, one can derive the policy π by always choosing the action with the highest Q-value:

$$\pi(s) = \underset{a \in A}{\operatorname{argmax}}(Q(s, a)) \tag{6}$$

Under these conditions, Q-learning should converge to an optimal Q-function

$$Q* = \pi(s) = \underset{a \in A}{\operatorname{argmax}}(Q(s; a)) \tag{7}$$

that returns the highest reward for any state-action tuple (s, a). Hence, in this way we establish an optimal policy $\pi*$.

4) Transfer learning: Machine learning and data mining techniques have been used in numerous real-world applications. An assumption of traditional machine learning methodologies is the training data and testing data are taken from the same domain, such that the input feature space and data distribution characteristics are the same. However, in some real-world machine learning scenarios, this assumption does not hold. There are cases where training data is expensive or difficult to collect. Therefore, there is a need to create high-performance learners trained with more easily obtained data from different domains. This methodology is referred to as transfer learning [24].

There is a hierarchical Bayesian framework for transfer in sequential decision making tasks of transferring two basic kinds of knowledge [1] [2].

In our paper, we uses meta-data (e.g., attribute-value pairs) associated with each task to learn the expected benefit of transfer given a source-target task pair. An example of such a metadata is given in [25].

5) Deep Learning: In reinforcement learning, an agent interacting with its environment is attempting to learn an optimal control policy. At each time step, the agent observes a state s, chooses an action a, receives a reward r, and transitions to a new state s'. Q-Learning is an approach to incrementally estimate the utility values of executing an action from a given state by continuously updating the Q-values using the following rule:

$$Q(s, a) = Q(s, a) + \alpha(r + \gamma \max_{a'} Q(s', a') - Q(s, a)) \tag{8}$$

Where $Q(s; a)$ denotes the utility of taking action a from state s. Q-learning can be directly extended to deep reinforcement learning by using a deep neural network function approximator $Q(s, a|\theta)$ for the Q-values, where are the weights of the neural network that parametrize the Q-values. We update the neural network weights by minimizing the loss function:

$$\mathcal{L}(s, a|\theta_i) = (r + \gamma \underset{a}{\operatorname{argmax}} Q(s', a|\theta_i) - Q(s, a|\theta_i))^2. \tag{9}$$

The backpropogation algorithm is used to update the network weights at iteration $i+1$ by performing the computation: $\theta_{i+1} = \theta_i + \alpha \nabla_\theta \mathcal{L}(\theta_i)$.

In this work, the stochastic optimization method ADAM is applied. Deep neural networks are used to approximate the value function. In addition, using a target Q-network to calculate the loss function significantly accelerates convergence. The experience replay dataset contains a fixed number of transition tuples in it that contain $(s; a; r; s')$ where r is the reward obtained by performing action a from state s, and s' is the state the agent transitions to after performing that action.

The experience tuples are sampled in mini batches, and are used to update the network. The experience replay have to prevent correlation between training samples, and helps to improve convergence. The target network in the loss function $Q(s, a|\theta)$ is kept fixed for a certain number of iterations and is updated periodically.

We outline outline an extenion of multi-agent deep reinforcement learning (MADRL) approach presented in [26]. We identify three major MADRL-related challenges and offer three solutions that make this approach possible.

The first challenge is to present the problem in such a way that it is possible to develop an effective implementation. In other words, the problem is to present the problem in such way, that it can be used by any number of agents without changing the deep Q-network architecture. To solve this problem, there have to be imposed several assumptions: time and space are discrete quantities, the agent's agent is 2D and the agents are divided into two groups of pursuers and evaders. Moreover, two types of agents are two competing groups (competing groups of agents).

These assumptions allow us to present the state of the global system as an image-like tensor. So that each image channel contains an agent and environmental information. This presentation allows us to take advantage of the convolutional neural networks that are proven to work well for image processing tasks [26].

6) Sequential Games: By highlighting some of the important issues introduced by learning in a multilingual environment, the traditional framework of game theory can not represent the complete complexity of learning with multiple agents. An important part of the problem is to make consistent decisions in a state of transition. This aspect can not be described by standard normal-form games, as they allow only stationary, stochastic features that depend solely on the actions of the players. That is why we are now looking at an expanded framework that summarizes both sequential games and MDP.

Introducing multiple agents in MDP significantly complicates the problem. Both rewards and transitions in the environment now depend on the actions of all agents that are present in the system. That is why all agents need to learn in a space for joint action. Moreover, as agents may have different goals, there may not exist an optimal solution that maximizes the rewards for all agents at the same time.

As the name suggests, Markov's game still implies that state transitions are branded, but both the probabilty of transition and the anticipated rewards now depend on the joint action of all agents. Markov's ganes can be seen as an extension of MDP to the case of many agents, as well as repetitive games to multiple state case.

B. Implementation:

We generate a discrete map with predefined dimensions. Then randomly put obstacles on the map. The next stage generates two lists: one with the pursuers and one with the prey. We study the impact of the number of pursuers and booty on the speed of reinforcement learning. We also investigate the impact of the number of obstacles on the speed of learning. And also we study the impact of magnitude of reward on non catching moves of pursuers on the speed of training.

In our case group of predator pursue a group of preys (intruders). So, as in a classic Pursue-evasion process we study our problem as a MDP task. The all members of either group act after all members of the other group have made their moves. So, we could describe our approach as a classic sequential game. Both pursuers and evader have a short range of view so they have to move continuously.

We define a stochastic behaviour of both of the groups imposing some additional rules. With a small probability α_{evader} will miss opportunity to move out and will give some handicap to the pursuer. From the other hand the pursuer with small probability $\alpha_{pursuer}$ will lose the evader from site and thus will give a chance to evader to evade.

In general, predators have a small negative reward for every empty step and the prey have small positive reward for every evasion. If a pursuer catch a prey the its reward increases considerably (at almost two orders of magnitude) and the prey's reward will be reduced by the same amount.

The groups are implemented by two lists: one for the predators and another one for the evaders. And a new prey is generated in random place on the map but out of sight of the pursuers. In our implementation, we claim that if the values of the use of MADRL will superapss MARL approach in mater of maximum reward. So, we will reach an optimal policy for a final number of epochs (steps) faster.

In order to speed up the training, it is good that the coefficients of the P matrix are somewhat closer to the desired policy. This can be achieved through a TL in a simpler environment (or just a part of the environment). The classic reinforcement learning consists of finding an optimal policy for the whole area with high details.

Our approach is based on following: In our case, group of predator pursue a group of preys (intruders).

- Loading the whole map and scraping all details but geometric obstacles
- Find a reinforcement learning solution for this plain map
- Use the MADRL and MARL to train both groups
- Load full map and use learned knowledge to study the impact of chosen factors in learning speed

Notation and transfer learning: Let G be the set of all possible tasks. Let $G_{source} \subset G$ be a set of source tasks for which the pursuers and evaders has already learned a policy and let $G_{target} \subset G$ be another set of target tasks that have to be learned by the agents. For each task

$$g_i \in G, let D_i in R^n \tag{10}$$

is a descriptor of features for the given agent(either pursuer or prey). We assume that g_i and D_i that are known to the all agents.

So, we define a target task $g_j \in G_{target}$, as the goal of the agents. In both groups this should lead to higher summary rewards.

We assume that for each pair of tasks (g_i, g_j) such that $g_i, g_j \in G_{source}$, the agents could reliable estimate $f_u(g_i, g_j)$. E.g. the pursuer "catch" a prey and respectively the evader "evades". So both groups of agents can use these similar policies estimates to predict the expected transfer benefit between tasks in G_{source} and tasks in G_{target}.

III. EXPERIMENTS AND RESULTS

We gather evidence to support the hypothesis that using the Deep Learning will significantly speed up the training process of Multi Agent Reinforcement Learning. Hence we claim that building of Multi Agent Deep Reinforcement Learning for Autonomous Agent behaviour building is more efficient that applying the MARL direct approach.

We perform the following experiment: for a given map we should find an optimal autonomous agent group behaviour. The map is described by its size nxn and complexity rate R_c.

We have two method: Multi Agent Reinforcement Learning and Multi Agent Deep Reinforcement Learning. And four cases:

- case study I - Study the impact of the number of pursuers and booty on the speed of reinforcement learning
- case study II - The impact of the number of obstacles on the speed of learning
- case study III -Impact of magnitude of reward on non catching moves of pursuers on the speed of training
- case study IV - The impact of the map size on the speed of learning

We study following algorithms:

- case I - Multi Agent Reinforcement Learning (MARL)
- case II - Multi Agent Deep Reinforcement Learning (MADRL)

We do the following task: for a given map we need to find optimal behaviour of pursuers. The agent's task is to travel on a chased the maximum preys for given amount of time. The environment is represented as a two-dimensional obstacle

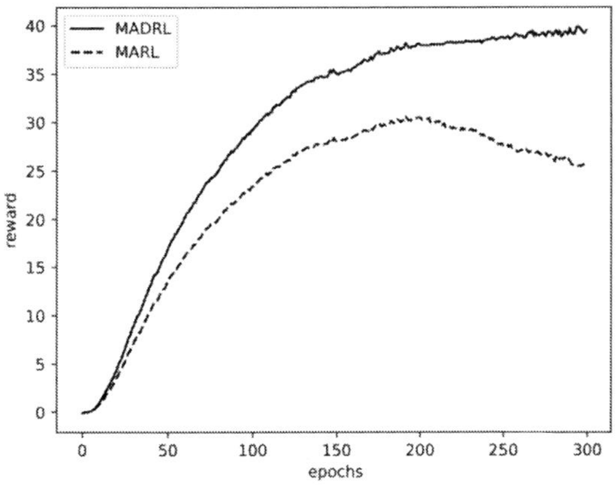

Fig. 1. We study the impact of the number of pursuers and booty on the speed of reinforcement learning.

map. The map is described by its size nxn and the rate of complexity R_c.

From Figure 1 one can see that when nuber of pursuers and preys are at the same magnitude then MADRL has a better performance than MARL.

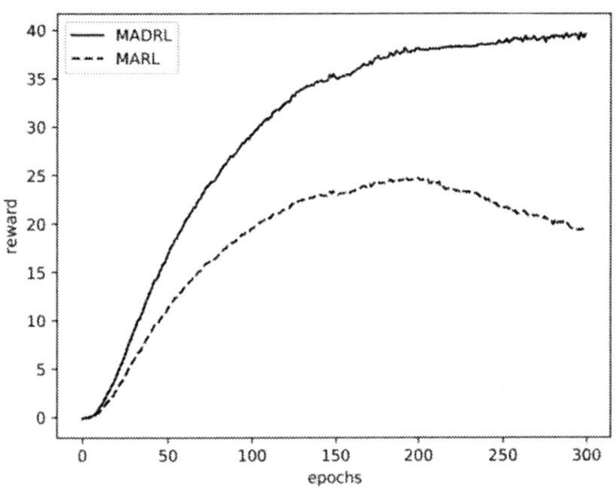

Fig. 2. We study the impact of the number of obstacles on the speed of learning.

hen the number of pursuers and prey is roughly the same then the MADRL is significantly better than the direct MARL. Moreover, with the rise in the number of ages, the quality of the gauze is significantly reduced while the deep approach is weakly affected by re-education. On a map similar to the first case, but with twice as many obstacles 1, the deep approach keeps practically the same total payout, while the direct approach has a considerably lower rewards. In the third case, there is a significant increase in the dispersion of the maximum reward MARL, while the deep training has a relatively stable dispersion.

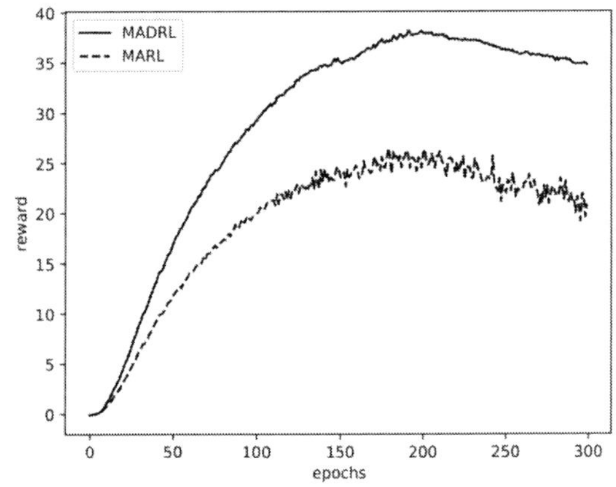

Fig. 3. We study impact of magnitude of reward on non catching moves of pursuers on the speed of training.

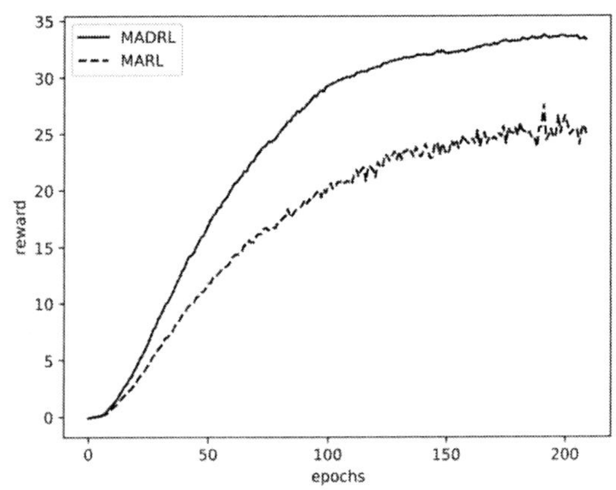

Fig. 4. We study the impact of the map size on the speed of learning.

From the Figure 4, it can be seen that for smaller maps the two approaches have a more productive performance.

IV. Conclusion and Future Work

The impact of different factors for building of Multi Agent behaviour is discussed in this paper. Two different approaches are presented: Multi Agent Reinforcement Learning and Multi Agent Deep Reinforcement Learning. The impact of four factors on Reinforcement Learning performance has studied. The summary reward is used as a measure of performance. In all case studies the Multi Agent Deep Reinforcement Learning demonstrate significantly better performance than Multi Agent Reinforcement Learning.

References

[1] A. Wilson, A. Fern, and P. Tadepalli, "Transfer learning in sequential decision problems: A hierarchical bayesian approach," in Proceedings of ICML Workshop on Unsupervised and Transfer Learning, 2012, pp. 217–227.

[2] A. Wilson, A. Fern, S. Ray, and P. Tadepalli, "Multi-task reinforcement learning: a hierarchical bayesian approach," in Proceedings of the 24th international conference on Machine learning. ACM, 2007, pp. 1015–1022.
[3] V. Mnih, K. Kavukcuoglu, D. Silver, A. A. Rusu, J. Veness, M. G. Bellemare, A. Graves, M. Riedmiller, A. K. Fidjeland, G. Ostrovski et al., "Human-level control through deep reinforcement learning," Nature, vol. 518, no. 7540, 2015, p. 529.
[4] Y. Li, "Deep reinforcement learning: An overview," arXiv preprint arXiv:1701.07274, 2017.
[5] T. P. Lillicrap, J. J. Hunt, A. Pritzel, N. Heess, T. Erez, Y. Tassa, D. Silver, and D. Wierstra, "Continuous control with deep reinforcement learning," arXiv preprint arXiv:1509.02971, 2015.
[6] T. D. Kulkarni, K. Narasimhan, A. Saeedi, and J. Tenenbaum, "Hierarchical deep reinforcement learning: Integrating temporal abstraction and intrinsic motivation," in Advances in neural information processing systems, 2016, pp. 3675–3683.
[7] R. B. Borie, C. A. Tovey, and S. Koenig, "Algorithms and complexity results for pursuit-evasion problems." in IJCAI, vol. 9, 2009, pp. 59–66.
[8] S. Barrett, P. Stone, and S. Kraus, "Empirical evaluation of ad hoc teamwork in the pursuit domain," in The 10th International Conference on Autonomous Agents and Multiagent Systems-Volume 2. International Foundation for Autonomous Agents and Multiagent Systems, 2011, pp. 567–574.
[9] I. Grondman, L. Busoniu, G. A. Lopes, and R. Babuska, "A survey of actor-critic reinforcement learning: Standard and natural policy gradients," IEEE Transactions on Systems, Man, and Cybernetics, Part C (Applications and Reviews), vol. 42, no. 6, 2012, pp. 1291–1307.
[10] C. Dimitrakakis, F. Jarboui, D. Parkes, and L. Seeman, "Multi-view Sequential Games: The Helper-Agent Problem," Feb. 2017, working paper or preprint. [Online]. Available: https://hal.archives-ouvertes.fr/hal-01408294
[11] P. J. Gmytrasiewicz and P. Doshi, "A framework for sequential planning in multi-agent settings." J. Artif. Intell. Res.(JAIR), vol. 24, 2005, pp. 49–79.
[12] P. Doshi and P. J. Gmytrasiewicz, "A framework for sequential planning in multi-agent settings," arXiv preprint arXiv:1109.2135, 2011.
[13] R. Smorodinsky and M. Tennenholtz, "Sequential information elicitation in multi-agent systems," in Proceedings of the 20th conference on Uncertainty in artificial intelligence. AUAI Press, 2004, pp. 528–535.
[14] Y. Han and P. Gmytrasiewicz, "Learning others' intentional models in multi-agent settings using interactive pomdps," in 28th Modern Artificial Intelligence and Cognitive Science Conference, MAICS 2017. MAICS, 2017.
[15] R. S. Sutton and A. G. Barto, Reinforcement learning: An introduction. MIT press Cambridge, 1998, vol. 1, no. 1.
[16] A. Nowé, P. Vrancx, and Y.-M. De Hauwere, Game theory and multi-agent reinforcement learning. Springer, 2012, pp. 441–470, chapter 14, pp. 441–470, in Wiering, M., Reinforcement Learning State-of-the-Art, ISBN: 978-3-642-44685-6.
[17] V. Markova, "Adaptive behaviour approach for autonomous mobile sensor agent," in Proceedings of the International Conference on Information Technologies (InfoTech-2012), 2012, pp. 1314–1023.
[18] ——, "Autonomous agent design based on jade framework," in Proceedings of the International Conference on Information Technologies (InfoTech-2013), 2013, pp. 19–20.
[19] V. Markova and V. Shopov, "An approach to build fuzzy cognitive map for time series," in Proceedings of the International Conference on Information Technologies (InfoTech-2014), 2014, pp. 207–211.
[20] M. Lanctot, V. Zambaldi, A. Gruslys, A. Lazaridou, J. Perolat, D. Silver, T. Graepel et al., "A unified game-theoretic approach to multiagent reinforcement learning," in Advances in Neural Information Processing Systems, 2017, pp. 4193–4206.
[21] M. J. Hausknecht, "Cooperation and communication in multiagent deep reinforcement learning," Ph.D. dissertation, 2016.
[22] L. Frommberger and D. Wolter, "Structural knowledge transfer by spatial abstraction for reinforcement learning agents," Adaptive Behavior, vol. 18, no. 6, 2010, pp. 507–525.
[23] C. J. C. H. Watkins, "Learning from delayed rewards," Ph.D. dissertation, King's College, Cambridge, 1989.
[24] K. Weiss, T. M. Khoshgoftaar, and D. Wang, "A survey of transfer learning," Journal of Big Data, vol. 3, no. 1, 2016, p. 9.
[25] J. Sinapov, S. Narvekar, M. Leonetti, and P. Stone, "Learning inter-task transferability in the absence of target task samples," in Proceedings of the 2015 International Conference on Autonomous Agents and Multiagent Systems. International Foundation for Autonomous Agents and Multiagent Systems, 2015, pp. 725–733.
[26] M. Egorov, "Multi-agent deep reinforcement learning," 2016, report. [Online]. Available: http://cs231n.stanford.edu/reports/2016/pdfs/

A Study of the Impact of Evolutionary Strategies on Performance of Reinforcement Learning Autonomous Agents

Ventseslav Shopov, Vanya Markova

Institute of Robotics
Bulgarian Academy of Sciences
Bulgaria
Email: vkshopov@yahoo.com, markovavanya@yahoo.com

Abstract—**Algorithms for evolutionary computation, are applied in reinforcement learning autonomous agent to discover high-performing reinforcement-learning policies. Evolutionary reinforcement-learning approaches allow the agent to find good representations and cope with partial environment observability. We have compared the performance of classic reinforcement learning and evolutionary augmented autonomous agent in area of sequential games.**

Index Terms—**Autonomous Agents; Deep Reinforcement Learning; Evolutionary Computation.**

I. INTRODUCTION

In recent years, the accuracy of machine learning methods has improved significantly thanks to progress in Reinforcement Learning and Deep Learning. Reinforcement Learning (RL) is a scientific area where the main topics are the autonomous learning and acting of an agent. So, agent is an environmental interacting autonomous entity, studying optimal politics for sequential decision-making in a wide range of areas both in the natural and social sciences [1]–[3].

The consistent structure in the modeling of different games has been dealt with in several theoretical and experimental studies [4] [5], which sets out strategies that summarize the results that would arise if cooperation or competition were chosen as one-off long play strategies.

Deep learning predominates in Reinforcement Learning over the past few years in games, robotics, natural language processing, and so on. We have seen breakthroughs like a deep Q-networks, AlphaGo, asynchronous methods and many others [6]–[8]. The integration of Reinforcement Learning and Neural Networks has a long history [9] and recent exciting achievements of deep learning [10] [11] leads to great benefits in areas of big data and data science. However, for several reward functions in RL, employing greedy optimization for a reward without any incentive mechanism can lead to sticking to a local minimum [12].

Evolutionary strategies are an approach that helps to find global minimums. A comprehensive overview of different Evolutionary Strategies techniques in the field of machine learning is given in the [13]. Several studies have been done so far [14] [15], however most of them consider the ES as an alternative to RL. If the agent greedily takes actions that maximize reward, the training data for the algorithm will be limited and it may not discover alternate strategies with larger payoffs. In this article we study, how evolutionary strategies could help us help to avoid getting into a local minimum in Reinforcement Learning training.

In our study, we combine Evolutionary Strategies as they were described in [13] and Deep Q-Networks [6]–[8] in Reinforcement Learning to explore the applicability and effectiveness of the agent learning in the field of Sequential Games. The main purpose of this study is to show that by guided exploration trough Evolutionary Strategies, the convergence of the learning process is faster. So the hypothesis in this study is that Deep Reinforcement Learning with Evolutionary Strategies exploration is more effective than Deep Reinforcement Learning with e-greedy exploration strategy.

This paper is organised as following, in Section2 we briefly describe some the underlying theory of Reinforcement Learning, Q-Learning and Deep Q Networks. In addition, we present the implementation of our approach. In Section 3 of our paper we describe the experiments and gather evidence to support our hypothesis.

II. METHODS AND MATERIALS

A. Theory

1) Reinforcement Learning: To solve sequential decision-making problems, the agent should learn about the optimal value of each action, defined as the expected amount of future rewards when taking this action and following the optimal policy afterwards. Under a given policyπ , the true value of an action a in a state s is

$$Q_{\pi}(s;a) = E[R_1 + \gamma R_2 + \dots |S_0 = s; A_0 = a;] \quad (1)$$

where $r \in [0;1]$ is a discount factor which trades off the importance of immediate and later rewards. The optimal value is then $Q_{\pi *}(s;a) = maxQ(s;a)$. An optimal policy can be easily learned from the optimal values by selecting in every state the highest valued action.

2) Q-Learning: The optimal action values can be derived through Q-learning [16] [17], a form of time learning. The real problems are too large to learn all the values of action in all states separately. Instead, we can learn a parametric value $Q(s; a; q_t)$. In this way, Q-learning values update the parameters after taking action A_t at S_t and observing the immediate reward R_{t+1} so that the resulting state S_{t+1} is then

$$q_{t+1} = q_t + \alpha(Y_t^Q - Q(S_t; A_t; q_t))\nabla_{q_t} Q(S_t; A_t; q_t) \quad (2)$$

where q is a scalar value and the target Y_t^Q is defined as

$$Y_t^Q = R_{t+1} + \gamma \max_a Q(S_{t+1}; a; q_t) \quad (3)$$

Updating the current value $Q(S_t; A_t; q_t)$ towards a target value Y_t^Q the agent apply stochastic gradient descent approach.

3) Deep Q Networks: Deep Q networks (DQN) are multilayered neural networks.These networks for a given state s outputs not a single action but a vector of action values $Q(s; a; q)$, where θ are the parameters of the network. If an action space containing m actions and state space is a n-dimensional vector, the neural network maps R^n to R^m. In addition in Deep Q networks there are target network [7], with parameters θ^-. This additional network is the same as the original network except that its parameters are copied every τ steps from the online network, so that then $\theta_t^- = t$, and are not changed on all other steps. So, the target used by DQN is then

$$Y_t^{DQN} = R_{t+1} + \gamma \max_a Q(S_{t+1}; a; \theta_t) \quad (4)$$

4) Double Q-learning: The max operator in standard Q-learning and DQN, in 2 and 4, uses the same values both to select and to evaluate an action. To prevent this overoptimistic value estimation we can decouple the selection from the evaluation. This is the idea behind Double Q-learning [18]. In the original Double Q-learning algorithm, two value functions are learned by assigning each experience randomly to update one of the two value functions, such that there are two sets of weights, and 0. For each update, one set of weights is used to determine the greedy policy and the other to determine its value. For a clear comparison, we can first untangle the selection and evaluation in Q-learning and rewrite its target 4 as

$$Y_t^Q = R_{t+1} + \gamma Q(S_{t+1}, max_a Q(S_{t+1}; a; q_t); q_t) \quad (5)$$

The Double Q-learning error can then be written as

$$Y_t^{DoubleQ} = R_{t+1} + \gamma Q(S_{t+1}, max_a Q(S_{t+1}; a; q_t); q_t) \quad (6)$$

5) Evolution Strategies: If the action values contain random errors uniformly distributed in an interval $[-\epsilon, epsilon]$ then each target is overestimated up to $\gamma\epsilon\frac{m-1}{m+1}$, where m is the number of actions [19]. This could leads to local optima. So, we need a new approach for achieving the exploration strategy that will lead us to a global optima. Such kind of algorithms are Evolution strategies.

Evolution strategies (ES) are a class of black box optimization algorithms inspired by natural evolution [20]. At every iteration (generation), a population of parameter vectors (genomes) is perturbed (mutated) and, optionally, recombined (merged) via crossover. The reward (fitness) of each resultant offspring is then evaluated according to some objective function. Some form of selection then ensures that individuals with higher reward tend to produce the individuals in the next generation, and the cycle repeats.

Recent work from OpenAI outlines a version of NES applied to standard RL benchmark problems [14]. We will refer to this variant simply as ES going forward. In their work, a fitness function $f()$ represents the stochastic reward experienced over a full episode of agent interaction, where θ is the parameters of a policy π.

$$\nabla_\phi E_{\theta\sim\phi}[f(\theta)] = \frac{1}{n}\sum_{i=1}^{n} f(\theta_t^i)\nabla_\phi \log p_\phi(\theta_t^i) \quad (7)$$

where n is the number of samples estimated per generation. The sample parameters in the neighborhood of t and determines the direction in which t must move to improve the expected reward. Instead of the baseline, the Evolutionary Strategy relies on a large number of samples n to reduce the variance of the gradient estimate. To avoid bias in the optimization process due to large scale of reward between domains, we follow the approach of [14] and rank-normalize $f(\theta_t^i)$ before taking the weighted sum.

Optimizing for reward only can often lead an agent to local optima. NS, however, avoids deception in the reward signal by ignoring reward altogether. Inspired by natures drive towards diversity, NS encourages policies to engage in notably different behaviors than those previously seen.

The algorithm encourages different behaviors by computing the novelty of the current policy with respect to previously generated policies and then encourages the population distribution to move towards areas of parameter space with high novelty. NS outperforms reward-based methods in maze and biped walking domains, which possess deceptive reward signals that attract agents to local optima [12].

Optimization if is performed only regarding the reward can lead the agent to local optima. With ensuring more exploration trough Novelty Search, however, avoids deception in signal rewards, ignoring the overall reward. Inspired by nature's desire for diversity, the novelty search approach encourages politics to behave differently than those that have been seen before. The algorithm encourages different types of behavior, calculating the novelty of the current policy for newly created samples, and then encouraging the population. We use the ES optimization to compute and follow the gradient of expected novelty [21]. Given an archive A and sampled parameters $\theta_t = \theta_{t+i}$, the gradient estimate can be computed:

$$\nabla_\phi E_{\theta\sim N(0,I)}[N(\theta_t + \sigma\epsilon, A)|A] = \frac{1}{n\sigma}\sum_{i=1}^{n} N(\theta_t^i, A)\epsilon_i \quad (8)$$

The gradient estimate shows how to change the parameters of our current policy increase the average novelty in the distribution of our parameters. We determine the progress of the gradient of A at the beginning of an iteration and is updated only when iteration is at the end. We add only a behavioral characteristic corresponding to each parameter vector, since adding these for each sample would cause the archive to be sipped and delay the calculation of the closest neighbors. To encourage extra diversity and reap the benefits of population surveys, we create two populations of agents that we will call followers as pursuers. Each agent, characterized by a unique identification number, is rewarded as being different from all previous agents in the archive (ancestors, other agents and ancestors of other agents). So, we have numerous agents in both populations, but we have not done a thorough analysis of how this variable parameter influences efficiency in different areas.

The choice of M depends on the domain, and that identifying which action is a beneficial for future research. We initialise the arbitrary parameters of M and, at each iteration, select one for updating. For our experiments, we choose which one to move from a discrete probability distribution as a function of the novelty of m. In particular, for each iteration of agent parameters, the probability of each being selected $P(m)$ normalized by the sum of novelty in all policies is calculated [21]:

$$P(\theta^m) = \frac{N(\theta^m, A)}{\sum_{j=1}^{M} N(\theta^j, A)} \tag{9}$$

After selecting a certain individual from the population, we compute the gradient of expected novelty with respect to current parameter vector, and perform an update step accordingly as it :

$$\theta_{t+1}^m \leftarrow \theta_t^m + \alpha \frac{1}{n\sigma} \sum_{i=1}^{n} N(\theta_t^i, A)\epsilon_i \tag{10}$$

Where n is the number of sampled perturbations to m_t , is the step size, and $i; mi = mt + i$, where $\theta_i \in N(0; I)$. Once the current parameter vector is updated, $b(mt + 1)$ is computed and added to the shared archive A.

B. Implementation:

We generate a discrete map with predefined dimensions. Then randomly place obstacles on the map. The next stage generates two lists: one with persecutors and one with prey. We study the influence of the number of pursuers and prey on the speed of learning learning. We also study the effect of the number of obstacles on the speed of learning. And also we study the influence of the amount of reward on the "elusive" movements of pursuers on the speed of training.

In our case, a group of predators pursues a group of victims (evaders). Since in the classic Pursue-evasion process, we study our problem as an MDP task. All members of both groups act after all members of the other group have committed their actions. Therefore, we could describe our approach as a classical sequential game. The pursuers and evaders have a short range of views, so they must move continuously. We determine the stochastic behavior of both groups imposing some additional rules. With a small probability α_{evader} will miss the opportunity to leave unnoticed and will give some handicap to the pursuer. On the other hand, the pursuer with a low probability $\alpha_{pursuer}$ "will lose" the evader from the site and, thus, give the prey a chance to evade.

In general, predators have a small negative reward for every "empty" step, and the victim has a small positive reward for every "evasion". If the pursuer "catches" prey, her reward is significantly increased (by almost two orders of magnitude), and the victim's reward will be reduced by the same amount. Groups are implemented on two lists: one for predators and one for evaders. When pursuers catch their victim a new prey is generated in a random place on the map, but out of the field of view of the pursuers.

In our case, a group of predators pursues a group of victims (malefactors) Classical reinforcement training consists in finding the best policy for the entire area with high details. Our approach is based on the following:

- Classical reinforcement training with e-greedy
- Reinforcement Learning with Evolutionary Strategy

III. Experiments and Results

We gather evidence to support the hypothesis that using the Evolutionary Strategy will significantly speed up the training process of Agent's Reinforcement Learning. Hence, we claim that building of Multi Agent Deep Reinforcement Learning with Evolutionary Strategies is more efficient than Classical reinforcement training with e-greedy.

We perform the following experiment: For a given, map we should find an optimal autonomous agent group behaviour. The map is described by its size nxn and complexity rate R_c.

We have two methods: Multi Agent Classic Reinforcement Learning with e-greedy exploration and Multi Agent Deep Reinforcement Learning with with Evolutionary Strategies. And two cases:

- case study I - we have the map with almost no obstacles
- case study II - we have map with big amount of obstacles

We do the following task: for a given map we need to find optimal behaviour of pursuers. The agent's task is to travel on a chased the maximum preys for given amount of time. The environment is represented as a two-dimensional obstacle map. The map is described by its size nxn and the rate of complexity Rc.

We have two cases: in the one case, we have a small number of obstacles, which leads to a low probability of stranding the pursuers. Thus, even at low e-greedy values, the learning process should quickly reach the maximum reward. On the other hand, we investigate the behavior of agents pursuing the preys in a map with a large number of obstacles. In this case, if a greedy strategy is used, it is highly probable that the learning process will get stuck at a local minimum.

In both cases, the number of hunters and loot is the same, arguing that the only difference is the number of obstacles. Hence, the difference between the two experiments is the probability of falling into a local minimum. From Figure

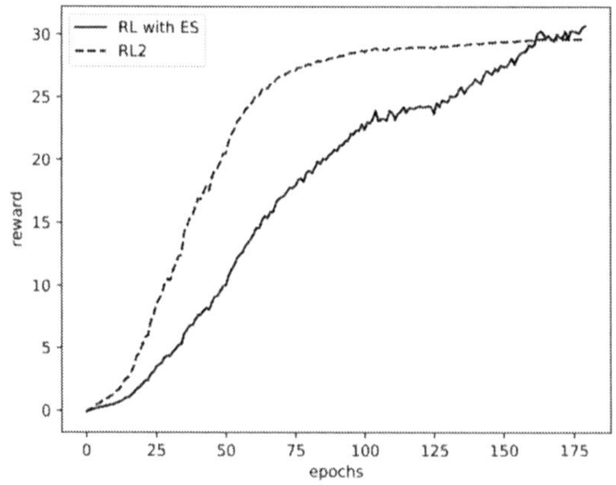

Fig. 1. We study the performance of Reinforcement Learning with Evolutionary Strategies(RL with ES) and classic Reinforcement Learning on map with low number of obstacles.

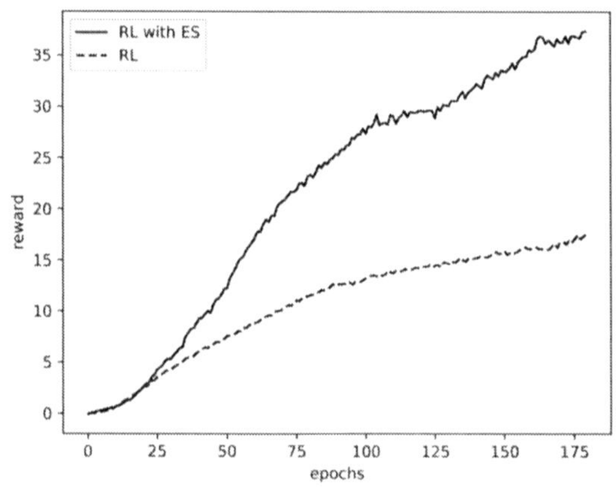

Fig. 2. We study the performance of Reinforcement Learning with Evolutionary Strategies(RL with ES) and classic Reinforcement Learning on map with big amount of obstacles.

1, it is believed that in maps with a low probability of trapping the pursuers and respectively a low probability of getting into a local minimum, the classic approach is better. However, in the event of a large number of obstacles (see Figure 2), the probability of jamming between the obstacles leads to a significantly higher probability of falling into a local minimum. In this case, the approach with evolutionary strategies is significantly better.

IV. Conclusion

The impact of different factors for building of Multi Agent behaviour is discussed in this paper. Two different approaches are presented: Multi Agent Reinforcement Learning (MARL) and Multi Agent Deep Reinforcement Learning (MADRL). The impact of four factors on Reinforcement Learning performance has studied. As a measure of performance is used the summary reward. In all case studies, the Multi Agent Deep Reinforcement Learning demonstrate significantly better performance than Multi Agent Reinforcement Learning.

References

[1] R. S. Sutton and A. G. Barto, Reinforcement learning: An introduction. MIT press Cambridge, 1998, vol. 1, no. 1.

[2] C. Szepesvári, "Algorithms for reinforcement learning," Synthesis lectures on artificial intelligence and machine learning, vol. 4, no. 1, 2010, pp. 1–103.

[3] D. P. Bertsekas, Dynamic programming and optimal control 3rd edition, volume II. Belmont, MA: Athena Scientific, 2011.

[4] W. E. Walsh, R. Das, G. Tesauro, and J. O. Kephart, "Analyzing complex strategic interactions in multi-agent systems," in In AAAI-03 Workshop on Game Theoretic and Decision Theoretic Agents, 2002, pp. 109–118.

[5] M. P. Wellman, J. Estelle, S. Singh, Y. Vorobeychik, C. Kiekintveld, and V. Soni, "Strategic interactions in a supply chain game," Computational Intelligence, vol. 21, no. 1, 2005, pp. 1–26.

[6] V. Mnih, A. P. Badia, M. Mirza, A. Graves, T. Lillicrap, T. Harley, D. Silver, and K. Kavukcuoglu, "Asynchronous methods for deep reinforcement learning," in International Conference on Machine Learning, 2016, pp. 1928–1937.

[7] V. Mnih, K. Kavukcuoglu, D. Silver, A. A. Rusu, J. Veness, M. G. Bellemare, A. Graves, M. Riedmiller, A. K. Fidjeland, G. Ostrovski et al., "Human-level control through deep reinforcement learning," Nature, vol. 518, no. 7540, 2015, pp. 529–538.

[8] D. Silver, A. Huang, C. J. Maddison, A. Guez, L. Sifre, G. Van Den Driessche, J. Schrittwieser, I. Antonoglou, V. Panneershelvam, M. Lanctot et al., "Mastering the game of go with deep neural networks and tree search," nature, vol. 529, no. 7587, 2016, pp. 484–489.

[9] J. Schmidhuber, "Deep learning in neural networks: An overview," Neural networks, vol. 61, 2015, pp. 85–117.

[10] Y. LeCun, Y. Bengio, and G. Hinton, "Deep learning," nature, vol. 521, no. 7553, 2015, pp. 436–442.

[11] I. Goodfellow, Y. Bengio, A. Courville, and Y. Bengio, Deep learning. MIT press Cambridge, 2016, vol. 1.

[12] J. Lehman and K. O. Stanley, "Novelty search and the problem with objectives," in Genetic programming theory and practice IX. Springer, 2011, pp. 37–56.

[13] D. E. Moriarty, A. C. Schultz, and J. J. Grefenstette, "Evolutionary algorithms for reinforcement learning," Journal of Artificial Intelligence Research, vol. 11, 1999, pp. 241–276.

[14] T. Salimans, J. Ho, X. Chen, and I. Sutskever, "Evolution strategies as a scalable alternative to reinforcement learning," arXiv preprint arXiv:1703.03864, 2017.

[15] F. P. Such, V. Madhavan, E. Conti, J. Lehman, K. O. Stanley, and J. Clune, "Deep neuroevolution: Genetic algorithms are a competitive alternative for training deep neural networks for reinforcement learning," arXiv preprint arXiv:1712.06567, 2017.

[16] C. J. Watkins and P. Dayan, "Q-learning," Machine learning, vol. 8, no. 3-4, 1992, pp. 279–292.

[17] C. J. C. H. Watkins, "Learning from delayed rewards," Ph.D. dissertation, King's College, Cambridge, 1989.

[18] H. Van Hasselt, A. Guez, and D. Silver, "Deep reinforcement learning with double q-learning." in AAAI, vol. 16, 2016, pp. 2094–2100.

[19] S. Thrun and A. Schwartz, "Issues in using function approximation for reinforcement learning," in Proceedings of the 1993 Connectionist Models Summer School. Hillsdale, NJ. Lawrence Erlbaum, 1993, pp. 255–264.

[20] I. Rechenberg, "Evolutionsstrategien," in Simulationsmethoden in der Medizin und Biologie. Springer, 1978, pp. 83–114.

[21] E. Conti, V. Madhavan, F. P. Such, J. Lehman, K. O. Stanley, and J. Clune, "Improving exploration in evolution strategies for deep reinforcement learning via a population of novelty-seeking agents," arXiv preprint arXiv:1712.06560, 2017.

Using Neural Networks to Evaluate the Intelligibility of the Speech in Voice over Internet Protocol

Angel Garabitov
Fakultät für deutsche Ingenieur- und Betriebswirtschaftsausbildung
TU – Sofia
Sofia, Bulgaria
e-mail: angel.garabitov@fdiba.tu-sofia.bg

Aleksandar Tsenov
Fakultät für deutsche Ingenieur- und Betriebswirtschaftsausbildung
TU – Sofia
Sofia, Bulgaria
e-mail: aleksandar.tsenov@fdiba.tu-sofia.bg

***Abstract* — An important and unresolved problem is the automatic quantification of voice quality. Many parameters affect the voice quality, but only subjective assessments are crucial. The article makes a proposal to create a solution for the prediction of subjective voice quality assessment. A neural network is used to evaluate the quality of Voice over IP (VoIP) solutions. Computational models of similarity, Musical Instrument Digital Interface (MIDI) analysis and Speech Processing Tools are used to assess intelligibility. Statistics techniques and algorithms are used for building neural networks. The end result is an analysis and an automated hypothesis about sound quality in the Mean Opinion Score (MOS) scale.**

Keywords-speach; VoIP; intelligibility; neural network.

I. INTRODUCTION

The intelligibility of speech is the defining characteristic of the speech transmission channel, since if the transmission channel does not provide complete comprehensibility of it, then its other advantages are of no importance - it is not suitable for operation. There is only one method for direct determination of the intelligibility characteristic: a statistical approach with a large number of participants (listeners and speakers). There are many attempts to create modern predictors of intelligibility. Two important issues exist with current intelligibility predictors. Many of these methods cannot reliably predict the effect of more advanced nonlinear signal processing algorithms on speech intelligibility. Typically, these measures are based on very complex auditory models or use average statistics of minutes of running speech, which makes it difficult on how to design new speech processing solutions in an optimal manner given such a measure.

To this end, we propose several new measures, which show good prediction results with the intelligibility of nonlinear processed speech. The newly proposed measures are of a low computational complexity and mathematically tractable, which make them suitable for optimization of new signal processing solutions, which aim for improving speech intelligibility.

An important and unresolved problem is the automatic quantification of voice quality. Many parameters influence the voice quality, but only subjective assessments are crucial. The article makes a proposal to create cost-effective and efficient solution for the prediction of subjective language quality assessment. A Multi Layered Perceptron (MLP) neural network is used as a "customer" to evaluate and predict the quality of VoIP solutions [1]- [3]. In Section 2, we will review the existing solutions. Then, we will propose a solution. After this, the dataset will be defined. In Sections 5 and 6, we will present the results and the conclusion.

II. RELATED WORKS

A number of measures have been proposed to predict speech intelligibility in the presence of background noise. Among these measures, the Articulation Index AI and Speech-Transmission Index STI are by far the most commonly used today for predicting speech intelligibility in noisy conditions. The AI measure was further refined to produce the speech intelligibility index STI. The STI measure is based on the idea that the intelligibility of speech depends on the proportion of spectral information that is audible to the listener and is computed by dividing the spectrum into 20 bands contributing equally to intelligibility and estimating the weighted average of the Signal-to-Noise Ratios SNRs in each band [1].

DIRAC PC software is a system used for measuring a wide range of room acoustical parameters. Based on the measurement and analysis of impulse responses, DIRAC supports a variety of measurement configurations. For accurate measurements according to the ISO 3382 standard, you can use the internally generated maximum-length sequence (MLS) or sweep signals through a loudspeaker sound source. Survey measurements are easily carried out using a small impulsive sound source, such as a blank pistol or even a balloon. Speech measurements can be carried out in compliance with the IEC 60268-16 standard [2], for male and female voices, through an artificial mouth-directional loudspeaker sound source or through direct injection into a sound system, taking into account the impact of background noise.

A lot of attempts have been made to find the direct connection between intelligibility of speech, on the one hand, characteristics of speech transmission routes and the conditions for its reception and transmission, on the other, but no acceptable results were obtained. Only through the formant theory this connection could be established [3].

III. Proposed Solution

We want to make an analogy between the melodic structure of tonal music and the understandability of speech. Using some approaches to determine the melodic structure to determine the possible speech intelligibility.

A melody is a linear succession of musical tones that the listener perceives as a single entity. In its most literal sense, a melody is a combination of pitch and rhythm. Melodies often consist of one or more musical phrases or motifs, and are usually repeated throughout a composition in various forms. Melodies may also be described by their melodic motion or the pitches or the intervals between pitches, pitch range, tension and release, continuity and coherence, cadence, and shape. All this is fully valid for the intelligibility of speech.

Before we do the analysis is necessary to invert the synthesis of speech process using formant synthesis and MIDI format. MIDI is a technical standard that describes a communications protocol and allows a wide variety of electronic musical instruments, computers and other audio devices to connect and communicate with one another [3]. MIDI carries event messages that specify notation, pitch and velocity (loudness or softness), control signals for parameters such as volume, vibrato, audio panning from left to right, cues in theatre, and clock signals that set and synchronize tempo between multiple devices.

MIDI file itself is simply an ordered series of 0s and 1s and this gave a way to analyze it using standard information theory. We will analyze MIDI sequences and perform a comparative analysis of audio signals (acoustic recordings) and symbolic representations, i.e., MIDI. By symbolic representation we mean a representation of speech as a set of notes, which is equivalent to music notation. This information is stored in MIDI files. We considered note numbers sequenced in the order of their appearance and regarding their exact onset times, durations and dynamics (so called MIDI velocities).

Formant synthesis is a special but important case of subtractive synthesis. Part of what makes the timbre of a voice or instrument consistent over a wide range of frequencies is the presence of fixed frequency peaks, called formants. These peaks stay in the same frequency range, independent of the actual pitch being produced by the voice or instrument. While there are many other factors that go into synthesizing a realistic timbre, the use of formants is one way to get reasonably accurate results.

Formants of speech sounds fill the entire frequency range from 150 to 7000 Hz. The average probability of occurrence of formants in this or that part of the range for each language is quite definite. The entire frequency range is divided into bands, so that in each of them the probability of occurrence of the formant was the same. They are defined for a number of languages. It turned out that with a sufficiently large amount of transmitted material, the probability of appearance of the formant obeys the additivity rule [4].

Our idea is to convert the speech recordings in MIDI format. To create a MIDI sequence for a speech recorded in audio format we must determine pitch, velocity and duration of each note being played and record these parameters into a sequence of MIDI events. We need to determine the order of sounds. It contains two parameters – height and the duration of the note. The structure of the sound can be analyzed mathematically by finding functions, which connect the parameters mentioned above. These functions are important for understanding the intelligibility of speech.

There are many such functions designed to analyze the melody of music [5]- [8]. We will use their ideas, but we will redesign the approach in order to analyze the sound of speech.

In brief, we want to turn the speech synthesis process to analyze speech intelligibility. There are two stages involved: sound to phonemes and phonemes to words.

The processing of this idea is too complicated; this is why we try to realize it with a neural network, because of its adaptive, deep learning capabilities and the ability to accurately separate highly correlated classes.

IV. Defining Dataset

A. *Mellaccent*

It calculates melodic accent salience according to Thomassen's model [9]. A musical accent can be defined as an increased prominence or noticeability associated with some note or chord.

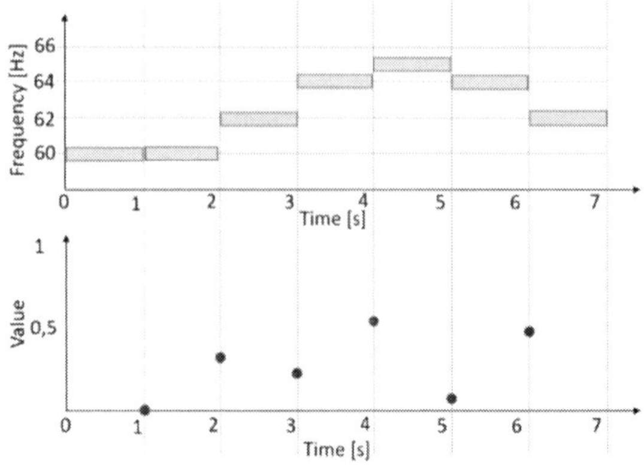

Figure 1. Melodic accent salience according to Thomassen's model

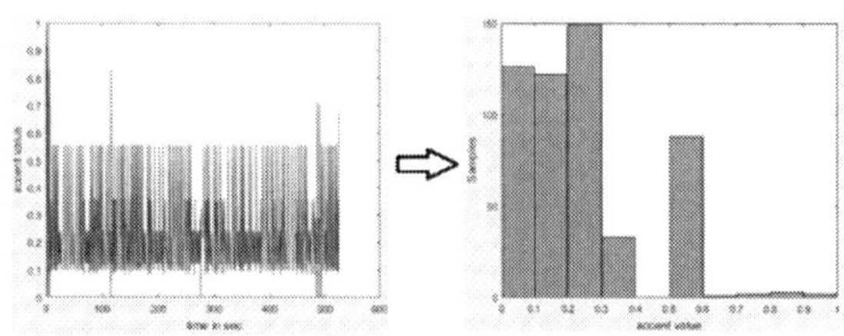

Figure 2. Mellaccent = [126, 122, 149, 33, 0, 88, 1, 2, 3, 2]

By "melodic accent" in Figure 1, music theorists mean accent arising from pitch-related changes such as changes of pitch height, pitch interval, or pitch contour. This model assigns melodic accents according to the possible melodic contours arising in 3-pitch windows. Accent values vary between 0 (no salience) and 1 (maximum salience) in figure

The resulting value is a vector. In order to be usable for us, we represent the output vector in the form of histogram. Each value of the bins is separate input parameter of the neuronal network.

B. Narmour proximity (pr) and consonance(co)

The model draws on the Gestalt based principles [6] of proximity, similarity, and good continuation and has been found to predict listeners' melodic expectancies. The model operates by looking at implicative intervals and realized intervals. The former creates implications for the melody's continuation and the next interval carries out its implications. The model contains five principles (Registral Direction, Intervallic Difference, Registral Return, Proximity, and Closure) that are each characterized by a specific rule describing the registral direction and the distance in pitch between successive tones. The principle of Registral Return, for example, refers to cases in which the second tone of the realized interval is within two semitones of the first tone of the implicative interval in Figures 3 and 4.

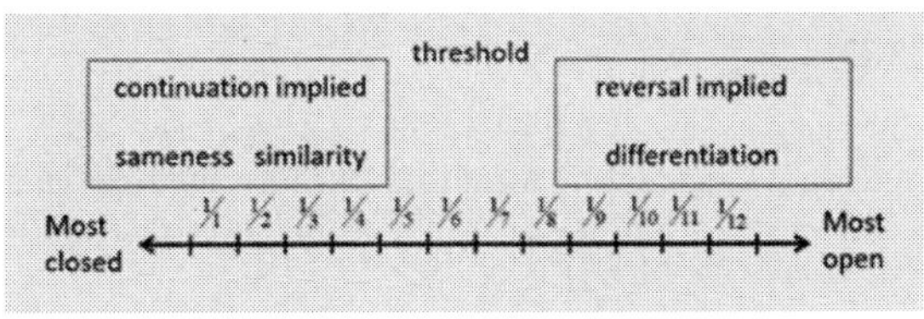

Figure 3. The Parametric Scale for Melodic Intervals

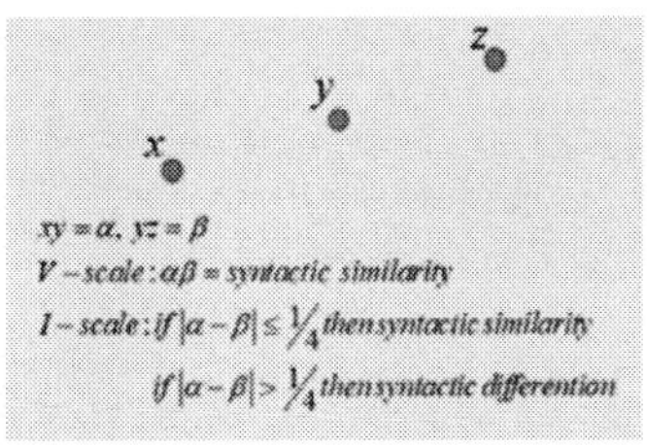

Figure 4. Cases of Intervallic Similarity and Differentiation

From all five principles, we used only Proximity and Consonance [6]. The output is also a vector and it is processed as above.

V. EXPERIMENTAL DATASET

We are using two criteria as identifier of the speech probe. They are in the form of vectors. Each value of the vector will be an input neuron of the neuronal network.

To investigate the impact of network defects is done with simulation of the loss of packets, the delay and jitter. Changing the parameters directly affects the quality and intelligibility of speech. The testing tool can be seen in Figure 5. In the performed experiment, we have collected 708 samples. Here we will perform some statistical processing of all these samples. The total count of input values is 23, and after removing a column containing only zeros the count is reduced to 22.

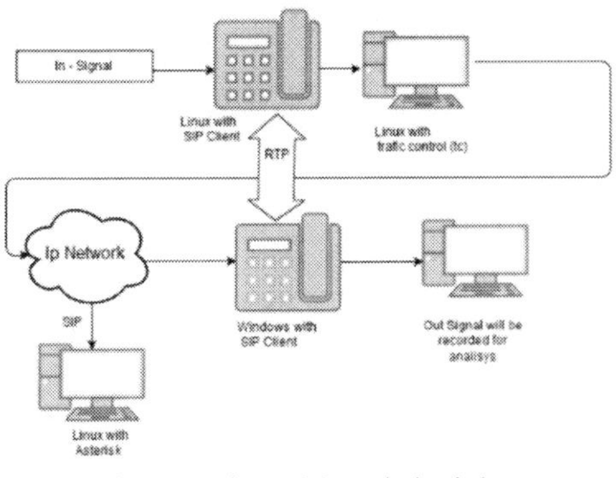

Figure 5. The used detwork simulation

A. Task description

The data set contains the parameters for creating the predictive model. It comprises a data matrix in which columns represent variables and rows represent samples.

The independent variable is 8 but in form of vectors. The total count of all input parameters will be 22 independent variables. The targets will be 8 dependent variables, representing the voice quality in MOS scale. Figure 6 shows the mean value of each input parameters depending of the target. Figure 7 shows the correlation between the parameters.

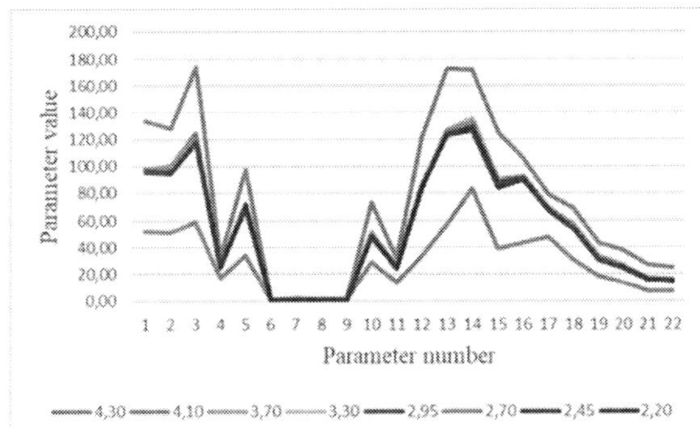

Figure 6. Data mean values

The number of layers in the neural network is two. The following table depicts the size of each layer and its corresponding activation function. The architecture of this neural network can be written as 22:22:8. Activation function in all layers is Logistic. The mathematical expression represented by the neural network can be written. It takes the inputs Mellaccent (1 – 9), NamorCo (1 – 5) and NamorPr (1 – 8), to produce the outputs in MOS (2,20 – 4,40). The NN errors are displayed in the next table.

TABLE I. ERRORS TABLE

	Training	Selection	Testing
Sum squared error	25.5304	12.253	10.9318
Mean squared error	0.0599305	0.0869006	0.0775302
Root mean squared error	0.244807	0.294789	0.278442
Normalized squared error	0.796492	0.788809	0.778646
Cross-entropy error	2.37538	2.3531	2.31614
Minkowski error	38.4993	17.0072	15.5343

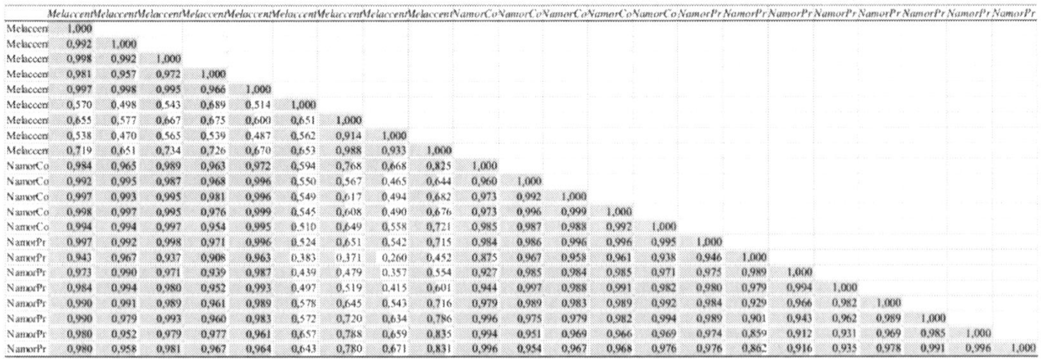

	Melaccent	Melaccent	Melaccent	Melaccent	Melaccent	Melaccent	Melaccent	Melaccent	Melaccent	NamorCo	NamorCo	NamorCo	NamorCo	NamorCo	NamorPr	NamorPr	NamorPr	NamorPr	NamorPr	NamorPr	NamorPr	NamorPr
Melaccen	1,000																					
Melaccen	0,992	1,000																				
Melaccen	0,998	0,992	1,000																			
Melaccen	0,981	0,957	0,972	1,000																		
Melaccen	0,997	0,998	0,995	0,966	1,000																	
Melaccen	0,570	0,498	0,543	0,689	0,514	1,000																
Melaccen	0,655	0,577	0,667	0,675	0,600	0,651	1,000															
Melaccen	0,538	0,470	0,565	0,539	0,487	0,562	0,914	1,000														
Melaccen	0,719	0,651	0,734	0,726	0,670	0,653	0,988	0,933	1,000													
NamorCo	0,984	0,965	0,989	0,963	0,972	0,594	0,768	0,668	0,825	1,000												
NamorCo	0,992	0,995	0,987	0,968	0,996	0,550	0,567	0,465	0,644	0,960	1,000											
NamorCo	0,997	0,993	0,995	0,981	0,996	0,549	0,617	0,494	0,682	0,973	0,992	1,000										
NamorCo	0,998	0,997	0,995	0,976	0,999	0,545	0,608	0,490	0,676	0,973	0,996	0,999	1,000									
NamorCo	0,994	0,994	0,997	0,954	0,995	0,510	0,649	0,558	0,721	0,985	0,987	0,988	0,992	1,000								
NamorPr	0,997	0,992	0,998	0,971	0,996	0,524	0,651	0,542	0,715	0,984	0,986	0,996	0,996	0,995	1,000							
NamorPr	0,943	0,967	0,937	0,908	0,963	0,383	0,371	0,260	0,452	0,875	0,967	0,958	0,961	0,938	0,946	1,000						
NamorPr	0,973	0,990	0,971	0,939	0,987	0,439	0,479	0,357	0,554	0,927	0,985	0,984	0,985	0,971	0,975	0,989	1,000					
NamorPr	0,984	0,994	0,980	0,952	0,993	0,497	0,519	0,415	0,601	0,944	0,997	0,988	0,991	0,982	0,980	0,979	0,994	1,000				
NamorPr	0,990	0,991	0,989	0,961	0,989	0,578	0,645	0,543	0,716	0,979	0,989	0,983	0,989	0,992	0,984	0,929	0,966	0,982	1,000			
NamorPr	0,990	0,979	0,993	0,960	0,983	0,572	0,720	0,634	0,786	0,996	0,975	0,979	0,982	0,994	0,989	0,901	0,943	0,962	0,989	1,000		
NamorPr	0,980	0,952	0,979	0,977	0,961	0,657	0,788	0,659	0,835	0,994	0,951	0,969	0,966	0,969	0,974	0,859	0,912	0,931	0,969	0,985	1,000	
NamorPr	0,980	0,958	0,981	0,967	0,964	0,643	0,780	0,671	0,831	0,996	0,954	0,967	0,968	0,976	0,976	0,862	0,916	0,935	0,978	0,991	0,996	1,000

Figure 7. Correlation between the parameters

For classification problems, the information is propagated in a feed-forward fashion through the scaling layer, the perceptron layers and the probabilistic layer.

The mathematical expression represented by the neural network can be written. It takes the inputs Mellaccent (1 – 9), NamorCo (1 – 5) and NamorPr (1 – 8), to produce the outputs in MOS. For classification problems, the information is propagated in a feed-forward fashion through the scaling layer, the perceptron layers and the probabilistic layer.

Table II contains the elements of the confusion matrix. 567 – Train samples; 141 (25%) – Test Samples. The correctly classified samples are 113, and the misclassified instances are 28. The obtained classification accuracy is calculated as 80%. Table II shows the classification results of the neuronal network according to the MOS scale:

TABLE II. PREDICTION MATRIX

		Predicted							
		4,3	*4,1*	*3,7*	*3,3*	*2,95*	*2,7*	*2,45*	*2,2*
Actual	*4,3*	18	0	0	0	0	0	0	0
	4,1	0	16	0	0	0	0	0	0
	3,7	0	0	17	0	1	0	0	1
	3,3	0	0	1	16	0	1	0	0
	2,95	0	0	0	1	11	0	1	3
	2,7	0	0	0	1	1	17	0	1
	2,45	1	2	1	4	2	1	11	0
	2,2	0	0	0	1	1	0	3	7

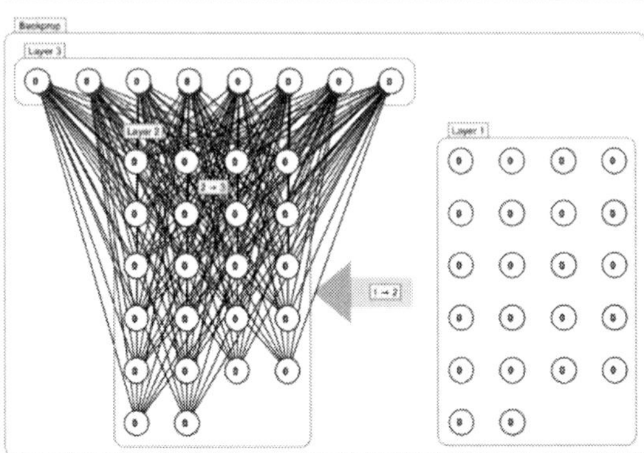

Figure 8. Experimental MLP topology

VI. CONCLUSION

MLP classification neural network with given criteria can be used to estimate voice quality according to MOS scale. The network is used as a "customer" to evaluate and predict the quality of VoIP solutions with about 80% successful predictions. An advantage of the method is the possibility of easy adjustment when changing the input parameters - only by means of re-training the MLP.

ACKNOWLEDGMENT

Research, the results of which are presented in this publication are funded by internal competition, TU-Sofia 2017, CONTRACT № 172PD0010-07 for a research project to help PhD

REFERENCES

[1] J. Ma, Y. Hu, and P.C. Loizou "Objective measures for predicting speech intelligibility in noisy," The Journal of the Acoustical Society of America, vol. 125, no. 5, pp. 3387–3405, 2009

[2] Xscala Sound & Vibration http://xscala.com/list/products/dirac-room-analysis-software/, retrieved: April, 2018

[3] M. A. Sapojnikov, Electoakustic. Moskva, Sviaz, 1978

[4] Ph. Burk, L. Polansky, D. Repetto, M. Roberts, and D. Rockmore, "Music and Computers", http://sites.music.columbia.edu/cmc/MusicAndComputers/chapter4/04_04.php, retrieved: April, 2018

[5] A. Swift, "A brief Introduction to MIDI," Imperial College of Science Technology and Medicine http://www.doc.ic.ac.uk/~nd/surprise_97/journal/vol1/aps2/, retrieved: April, 2018

[6] P. Toiviainen and T. Eerola, "miditoolbox (Midi toolbox) GitHub", https://github.com/miditoolbox/, retrieved: April, 2018

[7] M. Brookes, "VOICEBOX: Speech Processing Toolbox for MATLAB", http://www.ee.ic.ac.uk/hp/staff/dmb/voicebox/voicebox.html, retrieved: April, 2018

[8] E. Pampalk, "Computational Models of Music Similarity and their Applications in Music Information Retrieval," TU Wien, Wien, 2016

[9] J. Thomassen, "Melodic accent: Experiments and a tentative model," Journal of the Acoustical Society of America, vol. 71, no. 6, pp. 1598-1605, 1982

International Academy, Research,
and Industry Association (IARIA)
412 Derby Way
Wilmington, DE 19810

ISBN 978-1-5108-6543-3

9 781510 865433

CURRAN ASSOCIATES INC.
proceedings
.com

Fourteenth International Conference on Adaptive and Self-Adaptive Systems and Applications (ADAPTIVE 2022)

Held at ComputationWorld 2022

Barcelona, Spain
24-28 April 2022

IARIA